Tale of Nine Lives

Based on a true story

By

Sylvia Knopf

DEDICATION

This book is dedicated to Dr. Irvin Ingram.

Dr. Ingram was past president of the Arizona Veterinary Medical Association and he is currently on the Arizona Veterinary Medical Examining Board. The Arizona State Veterinary Association awarded the Veterinarian of the Year award to Dr. Ingram in 2002. He started All Creatures Animal Clinic in 1987.

In addition to helping in the Hurricane Katrina recovery, he has travelled to Africa, Tibetan refugee camps in India and to our own Hopi and Navaho Indian Nations to vaccinate and treat dogs and cats.

Contents

Preface

In Phoenix, Arizona, during the summertime, the blistering heat can deal a death sentence to animals.

This story is about two girls and the twists and turns they experienced while on the turbulent roller coaster ride of growing up. The cousins shared lessons and learned how to help save critters. They exhibited courage by challenging obstacles and their strong will to persevere no matter what the obstacles might be, taught them to never look back and only look forward.

This unusual animal adventure is based on true-life experiences and it teaches us all how rescuing animals can bring happiness, laughter, heartaches, compassion and unconditional love.

INTRODUCTION

Wow! What a ride! My name is Guadalupe and my heart was pounding, thumping away like thunder after these adventures. This story is about my two grandchildren, Breana and Kaila, and the real-life escapades with our furry friends.

An amazing story is about to unfold and it sparked magical kinships that will capture your imagination as you join us on these adventures!

Our love and quest for excitement allowed us to enjoy nature's abundant wildlife and blessed us with the power to heal.

Like baby sweet peas, Breana and Kaila started as fragile, soft new seedlings. As time passed, they encountered obstacles that enriched their lives and helped them grow into radiant, resilient flowers.

Breana and Kaila discovered that the compassion they had in their hearts for their best friend, the abandoned animal, was more than matched by the unconditional love they received in return.

On this mystical night, I gazed at the bewitching full moon hovering just above the dark horizon. In the moonlight, I thought back to a miracle and I will now tell you the story.

SK

GUADALUPE'S TREASURES

I

Nestled in the Arizona desert, a Spanish hacienda stood out in the midst of the Indian pueblos. A chili-colored dirt road led to this homestead inhabited by an abundance of wildlife. Many animals such as coyotes, bobcats, and rattlesnakes stalked the paths of this barren land.

An eccentric Grandma, who was a character full of spice and vigor, lived in this dwelling surrounded by spectacular and vast mountains. Nature and human life appeared to mirror each other as the mountains had wrinkles just like the Grandma. It was here that Grandma Guadalupe kept her family treasures, her grandchildren, amused during the summertime. Breana and Kaila could not help but notice the additions to Grandma's family as she was always rescuing animals that others had cruelly abandoned in the desert.

Breana, the eldest of the grandchildren lived with her grandmother. She was nearing her teenage years, tall for her age, lean as a rake and exuded a graceful appearance. She had a deep love for critters, along with an exuberance for life. Breana's compassion for others seemed to charm those around her. Her warm brown eyes, pale complexion and long dark braids brought Snow White to mind.

Kaila was a girl of eleven who lived with her parents nearby. She also had a bed in Breana's bedroom as she spent a lot of time with her cousin. This angelic maiden wore pigtails with blonde streaks entwined in her long brown hair. She liked wearing faded jeans and gauze blouses and she was accident prone from day one. Torn jeans, and scabs to match, came from falling countless times over objects that were visible to most people, but overlooked by her. In spite of that, Kaila radiated an aura that drew critters close to her.

The grandchildren had inherited Guadalupe's sixth sense toward animals. Guadalupe was a petite woman, in her late 50's. Her hair resembled a dry and brittle Brillo pad with her comb showing little interest in taming her kinks and knots. Her best friend 'Zap', a lightning bolt, permed her frazzled hair whenever the weather turned humid. She wore heirloom antique gold hoop earrings that had belonged to her mother. Her fashion style was very casual with 'off the wall' tee shirts and jeans. To brighten this up, Guadalupe accessorized her apparel with glitter paint and rhinestone studs. She felt these suited her image and the clothes reflected her spirit of adventure.

It was not her style to wear much make-up. A touch of blush and some lip-gloss always seemed to do the trick. The glossy look soothed her lips that looked chapped from eating too much hot, spicy stuff.

Her outlook on life was a jumble of chaotic optimism and she was not slow on coming forward with a cornucopia of ideas. Guadalupe had an intuitive nature toward animals and she was always on call caring for sick and orphaned critters that desperately needed her help.

One morning at the hacienda, Breana and Kaila awoke to a sudden cry from Guadalupe.

"Wake up my darlings; it's time for an adventure."
Every day at dawn, she carried out her ritual. Invigorated
by the early morning air, this majestic woman would lead
her grandchildren purposefully out into the desert. They
were looking for throwaway animals that had been
abandoned by their so-called masters. You may have
thought of her as strange, perhaps eccentric, but critters
could sense her compassion and they were naturally drawn
to her.

One particular gloomy day came to mind. They
were on a mission when they found several tiny kittens
burrowed underneath a shabby bush. They were tabbies and
all about two weeks old. Tabby cats have the markings of a
tiger, but are very docile and make good pets. Kaila was
cradling one of the kittens, when she noticed that it had six
toes on one paw. She looked at Breana and pointed to this
paw of the kitten and announced, "I'm going to name this
little guy, 'Big Foot.'

Breana grinned at her.

"That sounds fine by me."

With that remark, they continued on their mission
searching for more critters. The sun started to disappear
under the clouds when Guadalupe began to tire. She was
walking at a slow pace behind the girls when she called out,

6

"It's getting late, so let's call it a day. We need to take care of the kittens you're carrying."

"Okee-doke," replied the girls and they all headed back to the hacienda.

Arriving back at the hacienda, Breana noticed that Kaila was withdrawn and quiet. With her head bowed down, she walked quietly towards Breana's bedroom. Breana understood her cousin's sad feeling. Azul the wolf had been Kaila's loyal companion and best friend since she was born and she had crossed over the rainbow bridge with a guardian angel a few months earlier. Azul had been a family pet for 22 years. She was a pacer who wore a dirt path around Kaila's backyard, never uttering a bark, only a howl.

Thinking about the past, Breana remembered one particular incident with Azul. The wolf dog was always at Kaila's beckoning call, especially that last birthday when they shared a piece of party cake together.

Breana heard a muffled cry from the bedroom and quietly peeking in through the partially opened door she saw Kaila lying on her bed with her face buried in her pillow, sobbing.

"What's wrong Kaila?" Breana asked in a whisper. She knew why Kaila was crying and she was not surprised when her cousin had moments of despair and why her feelings went from deep sadness at her loss to happy memories of growing up with Azul. Kaila looked up at Breana with tears trickling down her cheek, revealing her iridescent birthmark.

"I want to see Grandma. Will you help me find her?" Kaila cried.

"Let's go," said Breana and grabbing her hand they marched together toward Grandma Guadalupe's sleeping quarters.

The girls' pace, slowed down to a tiptoeing, as they approached her room. Kaila looked at Breana,

"Do you think she's napping? Make sure you do not scare her. We don't want to give her a heart attack!" They both cackled together as they put their hands over their mouths, trying to be quiet.

Guadalupe had been dozing off to sleep and the whispering in the background woke her up. Dazed and half-asleep, she managed to sit up in bed, focusing on the direction of the voices. There stood the girls in the doorway. When Kaila saw Grandma Guadalupe, her feelings melted, causing a sudden outburst of tears that echoed throughout the room.

"What a sad little girl. What can I do to comfort you?" Guadalupe asked.

Kaila began whimpering, stuttering words—words that were hard to understand. "I..I.. want my Azul, I want my Azul to come and visit me. I miss her." Guadalupe knelt down to her level and stared into her glassy eyes, whispering, "I promise, I promise soon, very soon."

This moment called for action! Guadalupe's featherbrain suddenly snapped into gear. Kaila's birthday was rapidly approaching and one of Guadalupe's many talents included creating unique gifts for special occasions. She wondered, "Have I gone too far? Is this what you call madness to even think about giving my granddaughter a wolf puppy for her birthday?"

"More wild ideas whipping through this antique brain," thought Guadalupe.

"Girls let's go into the other room so I can make some phone calls. I'll be busy for a while, so would you please feed the animals for me?" Guadalupe asked. The girls responded, "Sure, we'll do it now."

Guadalupe thought to herself. "This isn't going to be a throwaway day. It's a day for resolution."

Several hours passed and after many phone calls to breeders, the search was over. There were wolf puppies in

9

Prescott. A trip up North to see the puppies would be required within the next couple of days.

Corriene was the only wolf breeder recommended by the Wildlife Refuge and she bred these beautiful creatures to keep the species alive. Guadalupe remembered watching a documentary on television about wolves, learning that they could so easily become extinct. Her eyes welled up and burning tears ran down her cheeks as she walked towards her kitchen window to view the sunset. Watching the iridescent sky gradually fade to darkness, she imagined a world where there was no wolf left to stir at sundown and no wolf left to howl at the moon.

Nightfall had taken over and all in the household were asleep, except Guadalupe. The steady drumming of rain splashing on the windows switched her brain into overload.

Finally captured by the sandman angel, Guadalupe slipped into dreamland, snoring, Zzzzzzz. The moon faded away, and the thinnest glimmer of light slowly crept above the horizon and soon the sun was peeping through the flurries of clouds. Nighttime had succumbed to daylight and a new adventure was about to begin…

Suddenly without warning, there was a crack and a boom of thunder. She jolted up and sitting in bed, she was overcome with excitement. The smell and aroma of rain aroused and tantalized her senses. The chimes rang from the grandfather clock and echoed throughout the house. This prompted her to gather her wits together and put her thoughts into gear. Now was the time to prepare for the trip to Prescott. Guadalupe made a call to Sheree, her daughter-in-law.

"I'll be dropping the girls off at the sitter's" Guadalupe said, "I should be there within the hour to pick you up."

The time had finally come. It was departure time and the journey had begun.

The tires whined and the engine hummed as they drove along the seemingly endless roadway to Prescott, and this only added to Guadalupe and Sheree's anxiety of what lay ahead for them. Dark green Juniper trees bordered the highway and the shimmering sun threw regimented shadows on to the road. As the miles sped by they could feel the temperature drop rapidly and looking out the window the view changed from Juniper trees to thick pines swaying in the wind. Strips of red clay adorned the mountainside. The traffic slowed to a turtle's pace with trailers and trucks all backed up. Sheree was losing her patience and in sheer exasperation at the delay, she cried out "When are we going to reach our dog-gone destination?"

The sky darkened and billowing dark clouds swirled over the trees changing the weather ominously. You could hear the fluting of the wind through the car windows. A cloudburst rumbled, a lightning bolt caught her eye and a downpour was imminent. Flickering patterns appeared on the windshield from the heavy rains, while the wipers clicked away in a vain attempt to clear the downpour.

An hour passed and then another thirty minutes …and finally the stormy weather subsided.

Guadalupe glanced at Sheree and said,

"We're almost there."

At last, after three hours of driving, they were approaching Prescott. Briefly glancing away from the highway, Sheree turned to look at Guadalupe and she asked, "Why are you grinning?"

Guadalupe's eyes creased as she wrinkled a smile and winked a knowing look. Sheree looked back onto the highway and cracked a grin herself wondering, "What am I in for now?" Remembering all those crazy adventures she had experienced with Guadalupe over the years, she thought that there was never a dull moment in her life. Will there be a wolf puppy for Kaila at the end of this journey?

12

Indeed, there would be and later that afternoon Sheree and Guadalupe made the return drive back home with an extra passenger.

Sheree and Guadalupe sat in the front, and sitting quietly in the back was Azara and she was adorable.

The prospect of having a new pet in the family made Guadalupe think back over the previous year and about the last pet to join the family. This was none other than a tiny kitten that weighed only four ounces. Come and join us on the roller coaster ride of twists and turns as we look back and tell you this amazing story …

THE ABANDONED KITTENS

II

It was a year ago when a very stormy day disrupted Katibelle's life. This day would change from a clear blue sky, to heavy clouds covering the horizon like a gray flannel blanket, with just a glimpse of blue peering through the cracks...

Katibelle had a coffee bean hue to her skin and she wore obscene tortoise shell sunglasses that no one but she dared to wear. The sunglasses pointed out and up on both sides like antennas, bringing in the forces of the cosmos, which was usually where her mind wandered. She worked at a factory in a rural area of South Phoenix. This company created cosmetics, sometimes thought of as clown make-up by women like Katibelle, who was not one to flaunt herself.

14

She was a mystical-minded person, a true nature lover seeking tranquility by sniffing the fragrance of wildflowers. This girl hiked many a mountain and jogged miles of desert trails. Katibelle admired the bright glowing light of the moon and the twinkling of stars at nightfall. This maiden had relished life, never missing a sunrise or sunset. Being adventurous, she was always ready to meet a challenge. She certainly was not the Cinderella type and some even thought of her as a "Plain-Jane." She was a single gal, in her early 20's, going to night school hoping to become a veterinarian technician. On the weekends, she volunteered at the Humane Society, a refuge for animals.

Katibelle was thin as straw and very tall, resembling a beanpole, which did not help her self-esteem. You could say the tortoise shell eyeglasses looked far too large for the size and shape of her face, but they truly enhanced her studious character. She always wore faded, baggy jeans, speckled with bleach stains accompanied by overly large tee shirts. She sourced these treasures at her favorite thrift shop and this helped stretch her limited budget. Yep, she had a tight budget but she knew she would dress the same even if she had a million bucks.

Clothes and makeup were of little consequence when animals needed assistance. Animals never cared if she did, or did not, wear eye shadow or if she forgot to tuck in her shirt in all the hustle and bustle of saving them. That was the nature of animals. They were always happy to see her staring through those wire cages. They knew her warmth would heal them. She spent her money on more important things, such as tidbits for the homeless critters. She certainly was no fancy person but her charm and bubbly personality was evident in her loyalty to friends and animals alike. In the eyes of friends, she sparkled like a flawless diamond.

The electronic time clock by the front door at the factory greeted all employees as they arrived and departed. Katibelle stamped her time card marking the end of her workday and feeling weary and brain dead she moaned quietly to herself as she looked down at the endless concrete floor.

"Why can't Ms. Carpet win over Mr. Hard Concrete to help rid me of these aches and pains?" She noticed her swollen feet from wearing shoes that were too tight and her feet ached from standing too long in the assembly line.

"Ouch!" Katibelle winced. An angry frown reflected her mood as she quickly threw open the old scratched and dented metal door. The blast furnace heat of the desert hit her when she stepped outdoors and this unrelenting wall of hot air showed no sympathy.

"You just never get used to the hot temperatures in the desert. Not a lick of rain for months." Katibelle thought.

She looked up at the deep blue sky, not even a tease of a cloud. The sun caused her to squint and wrinkle her brow, which blinded her eyes.

Suddenly, a dust devil brushed past her shoulder. Little did she know it at the time, but this gust of air from the desert foretold of an encounter that would soon change her life. Katibelle shrugged her shoulders and continued to follow the worn dirt path toward her car. Once again, this particular dust devil came from nowhere and pivoted, swirling around her, allowing the dusty breeze to surround her.

"Okay now, what is this, what's going on," she thought, "Normally, dust devils don't act this way. Is the heat getting to me? There are too many strange happenings for my liking."

The air was thick with dust, a warning that a storm was imminent. Her old Volkswagen Bug was parked a short distance away near an abandoned building and it was not difficult to spot. Its recent face-lift consisted of a neon purple paint job, which made it a snap to find. The steering wheel seemed to be mocking anyone who would dare to touch it without wearing gloves as the car's interior temperature baked to an intense heat of about 140 degrees Fahrenheit.

Katibelle's eyes fixed on the tumbleweeds, which gathered in heaps and mounds. She felt spellbound as the dust devils twirled like a ballerina, creating pathways in the dirt around the dilapidated and deserted factory next door. Katibelle felt her body tingling as she rushed to the car, while sweat dripped down her back forming wet blotches on her shirt. The sun's rays were intensely blinding and they seemed to bounce off the building's corrugated metal roof. In the windows, spider webs replaced the glass that had been shattered by angrily hurled stones. The run-down structure stood isolated in the middle of a dusty open field. Vast acres of cotton plants surrounded the building and these were dotted with endless snowy, powdery puffs.

In the far corner of the designated employee parking lot, a lone mesquite bush was growing in a crack on the asphalt. Out of the corner of her eye, Katibelle thought she saw a movement and the rustling of the bush! Mother Nature's swaying fingertips and glittering sunrays captivated her and drew her like a magnet towards the spindly bush. The dust devil reappeared, paused and made a lap around her. Ignoring its warning again, she carefully and slowly walked closer to the barren plant. Katibelle's waist length sun bleached hair swayed from side to side like a broom sweeping the floor. She crouched low to get a closer look, pushing the brittle sticks to one side and she could not believe her eyes! Nestled among the dead leaves and twigs, were clumps of brown fuzz. There was no sign of life and then there was a slight movement. Could they be field mice? No, the heads were not pointy. Katibelle spotted two Twinkie-sized kittens. Their slit eyes reminded her of newborn babes. The tiny belly of one of them gently eased up and down. This was difficult to see on the second one.

Katibelle looked around for their mother or any other surviving siblings. She thought to herself,

"It was very unusual for baby kittens to be left alone in such a remote area." She looked for paw prints, but there were none.

"How long have you been here?" Katibelle whispered to the kittens. One of the baby kittens bobbled its head giving a faint "meow" as if to tell her something was awry.

"Are they going to die?" she thought to herself, her mouth tasting of dust and feeling dry as a wad of cotton. This was enough to ignite a panic attack and a feeling of anxiety was about to upset her normal composure.

"What am I going to do?"

The blistering heat, while inconvenient to humans, can deal a quick death sentence to animals. She could not possibly leave these defenseless babies here to die! Ever so delicately, she hurriedly scooped them up in her clammy, damp hands, holding them close to her. It was amazing how easily they could both fit into the palm of her cupped hand. Her mind raced with uncertainty.

"What can I do? I have to save them!"

Katibelle ran quickly to her car, eager to shield them from the unforgiving heat. She pulled an old rag from the back seat and spread it across the sun-baked passenger seat where she laid the kittens down. Her eyes were squinting from the blinding sun as she fumbled for her sunglasses on the dashboard. With her vision restored, Katibelle put the car into first gear and sped off home. Even though it was a short trip, she feared the kittens would die.

"Home at last!" She said to herself as she pulled into her driveway.

She heaved a sigh of relief, followed by a heart flutter. Carefully, she carried the tiny tots into her bungalow. Katibelle walked down the hallway accompanied by the sound of the hardwood floor creaking. Once in the bedroom, she gently placed the newborns down. A soft, fluffy Indian blanket of earth tone colors lay draped across the bed and this blended in with the room's desert sand tones. It was soothing to the eye and it was indeed Katibelle's heaven.

She left the fragile bits of fuzz for only a moment, seeking out essentials for them. Several minutes had passed by when she tiptoed into the room carrying a box about the size of a book. It contained a baby bottle, eyedropper, mineral water and a towel.

"I'll first try to give them some liquid with an eyedropper," she whispered to herself.

She slowly picked up one kitten at a time in attempt to give them some fluids. Her efforts were to no avail. They would not drink! She carefully returned them to their warm, cuddly bed. Staring at the kittens, feeling helpless, she began muttering…

"These babes are too quiet!" Katibelle thought to herself. Assuming the little ones were sick, tears filled her eyes while she fumbled to make them comfortable.

Worried thoughts swirled through her mind as she stared at her reflection in the mirror. Her eyes burned from lack of sleep as she stifled a wide yawn…

"I'll have to take them to the vet's office in the morning."

She glanced at the clock on the nightstand, the fluorescent hands pointed to 11 p.m.

Katibelle had a premonition that tomorrow was going to be a heart-rending day.

Whenever dilemmas confronted the young woman, she would fantasize, looking through a pair of rose-colored glasses. What better way to maintain the illusion of hope! Her mind drifted into a honeycomb dream. The enchanted hour, midnight, would soon envelop Katibelle as she drifted off into a deep sleep.

The dream was always the same where daily reality inter-twined with visions and splendors of beauty. The fairy godmother appeared in her dream with her frail, slender fingertips grasping a magic wand, which pointed toward Katibelle. A spirited image, a very special and enchanted woman floated into the room wearing a white satin gown patterned with thousands of tiny pearls. She wore a crown embellished with red rubies and her long blond hair entwined with diamonds. In a puff, there was a flash, a bright yellow light, blinding to the naked eye. It engulfed her and transformed Katibelle into a beautiful, dazzling princess. She knew that she hardly resembled Miss America, but her dream was a release from reality.

Dawn snuck up quietly, showing hints of daylight. The man in the moon was faintly visible, cracking a smile to the stars as they winked back, flirting with their glowing friend before fading into daybreak.

From the depths of her sleep, she was woken up by a piercing screeching noise that penetrated through the bedroom window. She was frightened! She leaped out of bed.

"What is happening? Am I having a nightmare?" Thoughts raced through her mind.

A cold sweat had moistened her cotton nightgown, causing her to shiver when she ran barefoot toward the window. The electrifying screams were intense. She had to place the palms of her trembling hands over her ears to shut out the alien sounds. She pushed up hard on the wood pane window, causing a dry crunching noise. True to form, it always stuck when the humidity was high during a monsoon storm. She looked up when two large, brown malformed creatures swooped down toward her head. She yelled loudly, "Wow!... Ohh!... Go away; go back where you came from!"

"They look like prehistoric birds," she thought to herself, her eyes mirrored the size of saucers.

Still woozy from a deep sleep, her eyes focused onto what she thought to be hawks. Two of them, very large ones, had a wingspan of over three feet as they swirled in the wind around her cottage. Circling! Waiting! No, they were the 'Black Angels of Death!' Silent with their jet-black feathers and small beady eyes, the vultures picked up a foul scent.

"What a haunting experience to watch these extraordinary birds, so close to home," she thought.

"Why are they here? What do they want?"

Abruptly, her instinct alerted her to check on the kittens that were snuggled in a box lined with a soft cotton towel.

Katibelle's heart sank and her stomach tightened when she found one of the kittens had died during the night. Shocked and upset, she wiped the tears away from her red-rimmed eyes. Her hands turned cold and clammy from shock.

"This is my imagination! I must be having a nightmare. This can't be happening!" she cried in horror.

She soon realized it was real, very real! A minute passed in silence as she grieved and bowed her head. Her baby kitten had drifted off into a very long, deep sleep into the land of angels.

Her emotions flashed back to when she was four years old - a time when she confronted death for the first time. Katibelle held memories of the loss of her mother close to her heart. At the time, she was too young to understand the sad change in her life and even now as an adult, she still struggled to face the reality of her mother's death. Deep down in her heart she often wished her Mom's spirit would appear so they could share thoughts, fears and laughs together.

She tried to compose herself for the sake of the other kitten. Her crying tapered off into a soft sobbing. Fearing the other tot would meet the same fate she acted quickly. She hurriedly dressed while struggling with tears that welled up in her eyes before rushing her precious kitten to the animal clinic......

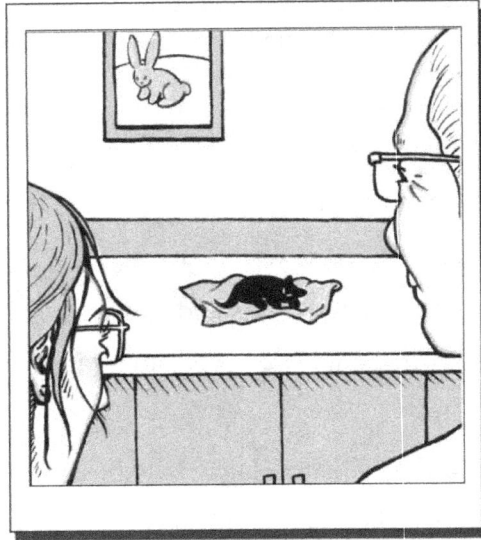

KATIBELLE AND THE ANIMAL HOSPITAL

III

Katibelle had a woeful look as she hurriedly walked into the Doc's office, cupping the tiny kitten in her hands. Shannon, the nurse, with her soft Spanish features and hazel-green eyes, had an aura of sensitivity as she quickly walked around the counter to greet Katibelle.

"Please let me help you," Shannon offered.

Katibelle, a regular client, described how she had found the abandoned kittens while the two of them walked together towards an examining room. Leaving her for only a second, the nurse peeked into the doctor's private office. He was at his desk speaking on the phone.

Shannon's waving hand caught Dr. Ingram's attention and he quickly finished his phone call. His sensitive eyes gleamed with warmth as he listened. He was a man of compassion, a distinguished shepherd. This man exuded competence.

"Excuse me, there's an emergency," she exclaimed. Within seconds, the doctor rushed to check on the baby kitten. Katibelle saw the empathy on his face and knew if anyone could save this little dear, it would be him.

Dr. Ingram took pride in his insight. And why not? After all, people talked for miles about his, "critter intuition," as though it were a separate entity that stood beside him in times of crisis, guiding him when all else seemed lost.

In Cubicle Three, the good doctor folded his arms across his chest staring down at the tiny kitten wrapped in a towel, lying on the stainless steel table before him. "Hey little tyke, where's your Mom? You're too young to be on your own," he said soothingly, and reached over to stroke the kitten, a pure black kitten, without a single white hair in his fur.

The little one purred loudly as he glanced at the doctor,

"Don't rub me too hard, I'm fragile. Sure don't wanna end up looking like a bald eagle."

Glancing back at Katibelle the Doc said, "Hi, you're back again! You're such an awesome person to bring this orphan to me."

"Centuries ago a pure black kitten was extremely rare," Dr. Ingram said to the young lady who stood across the stainless steel table from him.

She smiled painfully, "I know, I've never seen such a pure black kitten. He doesn't even have one white hair on him." Katibelle confirmed.

"They were all killed during the witch hunts," Dr. Ingram explained.

"Every cat that had even a trace of black on him was done away with. The pure black cats were actually hunted down all over the land."

"That's terrible," remarked Katibelle.

"That's fear and mob violence at its worst," Dr. Ingram explained. "And to see a pure black cat today is much more common, like a dime a dozen."

28

"Enough talking, now let's see what we have here," his voice was soft as he gently cupped the tiny creature in his hands. No response, only shaking—its tiny head bobbed since its neck was not yet sufficiently sturdy. He was too small to take a temperature and its heartbeat barely registered through his stethoscope. Dr. Ingram looked into its face, on to its closed eyes, and then checked under the chin and across its belly carefully for a trace of white fur. As a distraction, Katibelle scruffed the kitten's head while the doctor continued examining him.

"Truly exceptional," Dr. Ingram announced.

"To survive under a bush in the middle of the Arizona summer heat and to be found in the midst of thousands of cotton plants, is a miracle"... Katibelle was fidgeting, placing her fingers behind the tiny ears of the kitten as she massaged him.

The little guy stretched and yawned, clearly bored, thinking to himself,

"Why do humans rattle on and on, but yet make no sense. It's amazing they run the world, or at least they think they do,"

29

The kitten curled up in a ball without a care in the world and no idea of what might become of him.

The doctor turned the kitten over to examine the other side and exclaimed,

"AAH...Congratulations, you're a boy! What you want little guy, is a whole lot of TLC (Tender Loving Care), and I know just the Good Samaritan who will provide you with all the motherly devotion you could possibly need."
Turning to Katibelle, he carefully explained.

"Newborns need to be nurtured by their mom until they are self-sufficient. Mother's milk provides precious antibodies to help combat disease until they reach an age for vaccination. With some luck and his guardian angel at his side, he has a much better chance of surviving.

Looking down at his patient, Dr. Ingram eased up a bit of skin at the scruff of the kitten's neck. Like a baby mohawk, it stood there, holding to the imprint from his finger. Ever so slowly, it spread back across the kitten's neck. But the wrinkle remained, the sure sign of dehydration. The doc frowned as the flesh remained in a pinch. A deep sympathetic ache stirred inside him.

"This little soul is very fragile, dangerously dehydrated."

Dr. Ingram stared down at the pathetic kitten and motioned Katibelle to his side as he talked,

"When an animal is well hydrated the skin springs back like a rubber band."
He gently tugged at the kitten's skin again, showing her how the skin was sticking together looking as if it was glued. The baby kitten let out a squeaky "meow."

"The next 48 hours are crucial! The kitten will require round-the-clock feedings to keep him nourished. Even then, his chances for survival are slim. Try not to worry Katibelle, I know just the gal who's very experienced in caring for sick animals," reassured Dr. Ingram.

The emotional, downhearted gal sobbed when she looked down at the trembling bundle as the black fur-ball whined a meow.

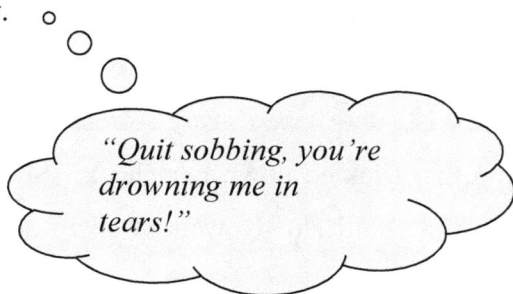

"Quit sobbing, you're drowning me in tears!"

There were tears spilling down her cheeks, sprinkling her blouse. Shaking her head, she nervously pushed her scraggly bangs to one side. She felt an anxiety attack beginning to surface, triggering an appetite for fingernails. She looked straight at the doctor, nervously munching on her pinky nail, talking all at the same time.

"Do whatever it takes. Please make sure he has a good home."

The kitten responded to Katibelle's voice and purred,

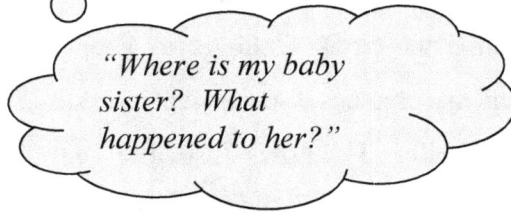

"Where is my baby sister? What happened to her?"

The baby tot had noticed the scent and the warmth of his sibling was absent.

Katibelle looked down at the baby tot whispering in his ear, "You're going to have the best home ever with someone who can care for you better than I can." Blowing a bubble kiss, she wiped away a translucent pearl-shaped teardrop that trickled down her cheek. She glanced back, one last time, and slowly walked away down the narrow corridor.

Katibelle went back to her everyday life. A new life was about to unfold for the baby kitten…

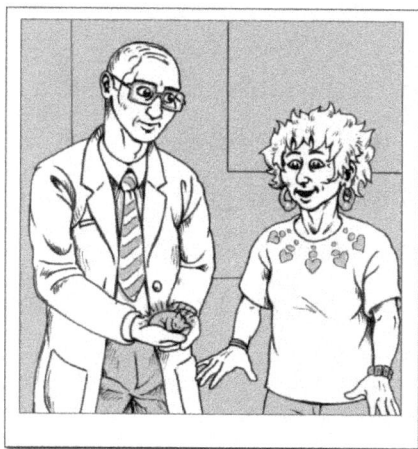

SAVING KITTY

IV

A deafening silence filled the room. Dr. Ingram crossed his arms across his chest and began weighing his options. His thoughts wandered freely, almost beyond his control, as to whether or not he should begin his tedious job of recovery care or…stopping in mid-thought, he called out to his assistant.

"Quick, call Guadalupe! If anyone has the magical powers and patience for this kitten, it's her."

"I already called her and she's on her way. I'm one step ahead of you, Doc!" winked his nurse.

Dr. Ingram stared at her with a strange, baffled look on his face.

"Do you, do you read minds for fun?" He stammered.

"Sure do," responded Shannon with a wry smile and brows arched high above her eyes.

"I knew you were going to ask me that," she replied, cracking a smile with a wink.

During the next hour, Dr. Ingram prepped the kitten for Guadalupe so she could take him home. The little guy was dehydrated, but otherwise healthy. His heart was the size of a pea and his spinal cord as fragile as a twig. He did not have any broken bones, only an army of fleas marching through his fuzz. The Doc wiped him off with a soft cloth, dabbing him ever so lightly with a mild insecticide to get rid of them. The annoying fleas were jumping all about—onto his sleeve, onto his coat, then onto the examining table and spreading out looking for their next meal ticket.

"Now isn't that better?" he asked his patient staring at the tiny babe. To his surprise, a faint meow rose up in answer as if to say,

"It's about time you got rid of these pesky fleas they were crawling all over me. The itch was driving me crazy."

34

"What was that you say--yes?" The doc responded. "Yes, I thought so, since you liked that so much, how about a drink?" he went on encouragingly.

Ever so delicately, he tried feeding his tiny patient with a doll bottle. Without warning, the kitten gagged! Dr. Ingram jerked back as he quickly lifted the kitten up to keep him from choking. Shaking his head with his lips moving,

"Oops! I guess not!" The formula sputtered onto his white coat staining it with dingy yellow spots.

"Dr. Ingram, Guadalupe's here," Shannon called from the reception area.

"Saved by the bell," he declared brushing off his jacket with a paper towel.

"Send her in, I'll be back in a jiffy." He walked out of the room carrying the pint-size kitten in the palm of his hand.

His mind wandered and he thought back to a much earlier incident involving Guadalupe.

"Remember that time when she rescued a dog that had been hit on the freeway, her quick thinking and emergency treatment on the spot before bringing the injured puppy here saved that one. This gal has a miraculous ability to heal animals."

35

His thoughts were interrupted when he heard Guadalupe burst into the examination room. With a bright smile, she glowed with enthusiasm at this new challenge. Her spirited energy was ready to take charge.

"I'm he-ere!" Guadalupe sang out. Looking around the examination room she found herself alone and she wondered,

"Where is everyone?"

Being in the vet's office filled her mind with memories of all the abused animals she had saved throughout the years. Like a mirror reflecting pictures, the past became the present with each episode flowing one into another.

One Spring day "Hooch" was found. A year old 'All-American' stray suffering from back and neck injuries, dragging his body and doing the best he could foraging for food. He was starving, dehydrated, bleeding and in no mood for a cuddle from a woman with tattered clothes and wearing no make-up. The indignity of it all, being saved by someone looking like that. Guadalupe knew right then, his pangs of hunger would vanish and he was all bark and no bite. He proudly tried to refuse her aid by snipping and spurting as deep as his parched throat could rumble. He imagined she might have food somewhere in one of her pockets. What were the odds of her not having a morsel or two? It was not as if he had other options lined up around the corner. Guadalupe sensed his gentle nature and refused to be barked down.

Then there was "Buddi," a hound mix that had been abandoned on a deserted university campus at the end of the school year. Cale, her son and his friend Demetria succeeded in saving this special girl. They were getting into their car, when screeching brakes and a loud blast of a horn startled them. The two of them saw the dog narrowly avoid being hit by the speeding car. Fortunately, Buddi became another one of Guadalupe's rescued creatures.

Perhaps the most unforgettable rescue was sweet "Zeus," a husky mix acting as mascot for a fraternity at the same university. That poor puppy's diet consisted of beer, and more beer with an occasional handful of scraps thrown in as an afterthought.

Cale knew Zeus was ill but his plea to help the Husky fell on deaf, uncaring ears. With a fierce determination, he set out to free him.

During the hustle and bustle of campus life, his fellow frats prepared for spring break. Making his move, he secretly snatched the puppy, quite willing to face his comrades and their unforgiving wrath. He took the mascot home with him.

When Guadalupe saw the puppy, she felt anger at the apparent abuse. Zeus was limping severely from malnourishment. She wondered if he would live and if there would be any permanent damage. With the combined efforts of Dr. Ingram's nutritional advice and Guadalupe's magical touch, Zeus grew stronger with each passing day.

Months later after convalescent care, Zeus flourished as if he was in paradise. With a shiny bright coat and sparkling eyes, he was surely not the same dog Cale had liberated. Luckily, Zeus showed no repercussions from having rickets.

Zeus was nicknamed "The Lifeguard." He was always on duty by the swimming pool, anxiously watching over the safety of all the family.

A miraculous event took place when Guadalupe's granddaughters, Breana and Kaila made friends with an alley cat they came to know as 'Simezer.'(pronounced si-mee- zer.) He was hungry and appeared to have been mistreated. His matted coat barely covered the sores that were oozing from infection.

Guadalupe thought of the many lost, neglected and abused animals in the city she had come across. She could remember them all, trying not to think about the unfortunate ones that had been impossible to save.

Suddenly, Dr. Ingram entered the examining room. "Guadalupe," he called out in a low deep voice. His melodramatic flair startled her back to reality.

"What's up doc?" exclaimed Guadalupe, as she jumped up from her chair.

"May I introduce you to your new friend? Another fine addition to your, already abundant menagerie of furry and feathered friends!" chuckled Dr. Ingram.

Guadalupe's eyes, like luminous lasers, zeroed in on the little black kitten that resembled a drowned mouse, cupped in Dr. Ingram's hand. She felt a mother's love swell from her heart and her heartbeat briefly fluttered.

"My goodness, what do we have here? You are so teeny and oh, so precious! Come here my little one," she whispered softly as the kitten replied with a growl

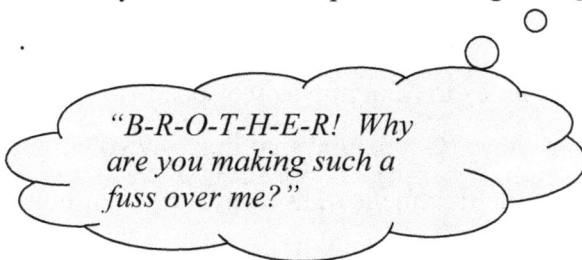

"B-R-O-T-H-E-R! Why are you making such a fuss over me?"

Guadalupe had a magical touch with cats and she carefully held the kitten while staring down at the tiny fur ball, fluttering her eyelashes. The kitten's weak paw reached toward her face trying to catch the butterfly kiss. This gesture created an immediate bonding as she cradled him.

"What a challenge!"

"This will be my first experience caring for a newborn kitten," expressed Guadalupe.

"This mission calls for a vigilant watch!"

Dr. Ingram explained, "He'll need to be fed small amounts of formula and mineral water with an eyedropper, every 15 to 30 minutes around the clock until he can drink from a bottle."

"Our biggest concern with him is dehydration. He's dry as a bone inside and if we can't get him juiced up, we'll lose him."

"No intravenous feedings?" asked Guadalupe.

"He's entirely too small to use any kind of needle," Dr Ingram contended. "His little blood veins are the size of a fishing line and shriveling up as we speak."

Poor baby, "Guadalupe said in a low voice.

"Start the treatment right away, "he continued, "It's important to check on his vital signs regularly, every few hours."

Glancing down at the kitten, his face saddened, but changed quickly to a smile as he realized he would be putting this little critter's life into the best of hands.

"You think this is a challenge? Heh! You'll see," laughed Guadalupe, happy as a lark. Being a great believer in eye contact, she stared directly through the good doctor's wire rim glasses, beyond the smudge prints and into his pebble, brown eyes.

"Doc, just hold onto my kitten, while I go and quickly buy the supplies I need for him." Guadalupe cried out.

She rushed out of the room, flashing a beaming smile, setting a pace to fetch all the lifesaving commodities she would need to accomplish this mission. Guadalupe climbed into her car, accelerated quickly and hurriedly flew to the pet emporium. Upon arrival at the store, she scurried up and down the aisles gathering the items she needed. Her shopping list consisted of kitten formula, mineral water, a small animal bottle, an eyedropper, baby wipes and cotton balls...

She thought to herself, "job well done,"

"I'm finished!" She walked out of the pet center exhausted, smiling to herself that the previous hour had been spent 'power shopping'!

SURPRISE

V

Guadalupe fiddled with the radio dial until she found the 50's music she liked to listen to on special days. The volume was at full blast as she drove home to quickly set up a nursing station for the kitten. Her fingers tapped on the steering wheel to the beat of the music that never failed to give her an adrenalin rush. Her spirit was up for a challenge. She was ecstatic!

Suddenly Guadalupe remembered tomorrow was Breana's birthday.

"I've got a wild idea! I'll ask Sheree to take Breana and Kaila to pick up the kitten from Dr. Ingram's office while I finish up here. "

She thought, "They are such bright girls and they always have their noses stuck in a book. Their brains are like sponges, absorbing everything about Mother Nature's extended family. I am sure they will become vets someday or have something to do with caring for animals. Breana has a natural instinct for helping animals and this has been apparent since the day she was born. Kaila was unusual as she had a faint strawberry birthmark. It resembled the shape of a kitten's paw print, embossed on her right cheek, just below her eye. The family lore was that the birthmark appeared after an angel had kissed her soon after birth. Not noticeable to the human eye at a glance, the birthmark glowed whenever she cried as a baby or became ill with a fever. Strangely enough, at an early age, she shared a unique rapport with many unwanted critters. She was a caretaker for animals and both the girls love surprises!" Guadalupe smiled warmly, imagining the look of pure delight on her granddaughters' gleaming faces. This will be a fun surprise, one of a kind, a special birthday present for Breana and a special surprise for Kaila!"

The hacienda came into view as her car skidded, swaying back and forth on the chili-colored dirt road. Hitting a pothole jolted Guadalupe's attention back into the real world.

"Oh no, not again!" She cried as her foot slammed on the brakes. The car skidded... tires squealed... and she only narrowly avoided hitting her casa by a few inches before coming to a screeching halt. Her heart still throbbing, she caught her breath and sighed with relief. Staring at the garage door, she pressed the button on the opener, waiting as the double door rose ever so slowly, creaking and grinding all the way up.

She cried aloud, "stupid door! Why do you go up sooo sl-owly?"

"It's surely not from when I backed out without opening the garage door first?" She cackled to herself, as the goofy episode replayed itself in her mind.

"Another 'not so cool' move on my part," thought Guadalupe shaking her head.

Guadalupe picked up her denim bag quickly and dashed into the house. That old denim bag had seen better days, but it gave her a sense of security like that of an old friend. She walked briskly into the house and not paying attention, she stepped in the cat's litter box, crunch...crunch... Feeling a bit anxious about her new idea, she grabbed the phone. It slipped out of her hand and dropped to the floor. Picking it up, she methodically speed dialed, punching #2, and eagerly waited for Sheree to respond. Ring…Ringing…Ring…The phone sang out.

"Hurry up Sheree, answer the phone!" her heart pounded with anticipation. Finally, after the fifth ring….

"Hello," Sheree casually answered in her natural monotone voice. She was a slender, perky blonde-haired lady with eyes the precise shade of a clear summer blue sky. She was a light-hearted person with genuine love for all animals.

"Sheree, guess who? It's me."

"I need a favor from you," blurted Guadalupe. Pacing, she held the phone upside down to her ear and acted like a giddy kid. Her voice sounded out of breath, causing her to wheeze like Snufelufagus.

"Sure," Sheree replied.

"What is it? What do you want? Is everything okay?" she asked, sensing the urgency in Guadalupe's voice.

"I know Breana is with you guys, would you please take the girls to the All Creatures Animal Clinic to pick up a package? It's a surprise birthday present for Breana, so you have to promise me you won't let her peek."
Sheree let out a slight snicker.

45

"Hurry!   This   needs   to   be   done,   pronto!'"
Guadalupe said.

"Okay, okay," Sheree smiled and rolled her eyes, as she hung up the telephone.

"Oh good grief!" she turned around and walked toward the back door looking for the girls. Peering through the glass arcadia door, she saw them in the backyard playing with Azul, the wolf who relished the attention.

"Kaila," she called briskly.

"Come put your shoes on, we have to go, **now**! Breana, you too" Grandma has a surprise package waiting for you at the animal clinic."

"What is it?" Kaila asked. The excitement caused her birthmark to glow with the rush of adrenalin and the paw print became faintly visible on her cheek.

"Never mind, just hurry up young lady! We're out of here in five minutes, Breana are you ready?" Sheree asked emphatically.

"Wait a minute, cried Kaila, as her birthmark came into view.

"I'm playing with Azul; she's lonely without me."

"Kailatola,----Move it!----Now!!" Sheree snapped, creating a severe frost condition between mother and daughter.

46

She knew by her mother's, icy-toned voice; she was serious! Kaila cranked herself into high gear, and ran to fetch her shoes in the bedroom with Breana running behind. As usual, Kaila was barefooted. In her world, it was only necessary to wear shoes when going to school. Her mom was in the truck impatiently waiting, as Kaila hastily skipped to the Bronco with shoes and Breana in tow.

"It's about time!" Sheree gasped in exasperation.

"This trip to the veterinarian clinic is all about you two."

Kaila and Breana thought for a moment.

"What do you mean, it's all about us?" Kaila asked wrinkling her nose, looking directly into her mom's eyes.

"You'll see when we get there," said Sheree.

They rode in silence as the scenery changed from neighborhood houses to office buildings and shops. Traffic lights flickered at every block.

"What's Grandma up to this time?" Breana finally spoke up. "She's always doing something weird."

Wrapped up in her own thoughts, Kaila quietly stared out of the rear window, before she started saying.

"Grandma's pastime has always been conjuring up surprises. You just never know what she'll think of next."

Breana sat slouched down in the back seat, biting her lower lip, her hand cupped under her chin, deep in thought....

"Hmmm....Let's see. It's at the animal clinic, so it must have something to do with critters," Breana thought aloud hoping this would uncover some clues.

"We are always rescuing animals, maybe it is something I can use on my 'patients'...or perhaps a vet book...or better yet, some old lab equipment so I can set up my own animal hospital...Yeah, that'd be cool! What fun this could be!"

"Daydreaming again?" Sheree said, glancing back as she gently coaxed Breana back to reality out of her pipedream.

"Are we almost there?" Kaila cried anxiously.

The suspense was driving her wacky, causing the image of the paw print on her cheek to glow a deep scarlet color. The birthmark puffed up shimmering like a 3-D hologram.

"Take a look, take a good look out your window," laughed her Mom.

"We're here!" Kaila cried out with glee, clapping her hands.

They jumped out of the car with Sheree trailing close behind. The three of them entered the vet's office with smiles on their faces, bubbling with excitement.

"Howdy Ms. Kaila and Ms. Breana." said Shannon in her 'Southern' accent. She had been Dr. Ingram's receptionist for so long, her presence became that of a permanent fixture.

This bubbly woman was always cheerful and warmhearted to all who walked through the door. Her overwhelming scent of rosewater lingered as she breezed past you and you could imagine that you were standing in a flower garden. She always wore pinafore blouses and pleated skirts that made her look larger than she actually was. Her 1950's bouffant hairdo sported spit curls and the curly ringlets fell loosely around her ears. Her ears in turn had dangling doorknobs for earrings and these accentuated her own personal style. She looked as though she had stepped out of a faded photograph of the early rock and roll music era. One only had to look at Shannon to know she was from days gone by.

"I spoke with Ms. Guadalupe on the telephone. She asked me to give y'all a basket of great interest to both of you. Now y'all, wait just one minute, while I fetch the surprise. I'll be back before you can say 'Kalamazoo'…"

Shannon walked awkwardly, wearing foot-pinching, pointed-toe high heels. Clicking with each step, she vanished down the hallway.

"How silly she looked," Sheree thought to herself.

"Thank you" Kaila cried out to Shannon before quickly diverting her attention to repeating, "KALLA-MA-ZOO-OO!   ...Kallamazoo-Kallamazoo-Kallamazoo-Kallama.." Time passed slowly...

Finally, after 10 minutes, the echoing sound of clicking high heels gradually grew louder and louder announcing her entrance as Shannon pushed open the door.

"Okay, Okay. Hush now, I'm back," clearly acknowledging that she had heard the entire racket Kaila was making in the waiting room.

"What is it? What can it be!" stuttered Breana.

Shannon had returned with a pink and yellow basket trimmed with a last-minute big red bow, a final touch only Shannon could think of.

"What's that? An Easter Basket?" The girls exclaimed, looking puzzled.

"But, but, it's July!" Kaila remarked.

"Besides, it...it's not Easter, it's my birthday!" Breana stuttered looking dumbstruck.

"Mom, do you suppose poor Grandma has gone completely loco-in-the-cabesa?" {Spanish word for 'crazy in the head'}. Peering wide-eyed at her mom, Kaila talked as she twirled her hair around her finger along the side of her head.

Shannon placed the basket gently in Breana's hands.

"Now Ms. Kaila and Ms. Breana, be very careful with this package!"

"It's Fragile! It is extremely fragile. Make sure you handle it with care," she said as she stepped back into the reception area and continued talking, "Ms. Guadalupe said no peekin' and she means no peekin'."

"Oh, thanks, a bunch," Kaila faked a smile, slowly hesitating and not saying anything further. She was dumbfounded as to what the surprise could be.

"Bye, see you soon," said Sheree.

The girls walked out with Sheree and they had stunned expressions on their faces.

They quickly headed for the car parked only a hop, skip, and a jump away.

"Hurry Mom, open the door. It's hot!" gasped Kaila. Sheree opened the car door and Kaila and Breana climbed in quickly, carefully holding the mystery basket with the bow on top.

"Mom, turn on the air conditioner. Please. It's hot back here!" Kaila whined impatiently, waiting for the car to cool down.

Sheree reached over to turn on the air conditioning controls. First a gush of stale, hot air flushed out from the vent, then the temperature changed to crisp cold air and the car cooled off quickly.

"What is it?" asked Breana.

"Why do you think it's so fragile?" asked Kaila.

"Is it alive?" Breana inquired.

"I don't know. Maybe it's Easter eggs." Sheree said jokingly.

"Mommm"…Kaila moaned… She did not find this amusing.

"Now, don't peek either of you!" Sheree said with a bit of teasing in her voice.

"AAWW, why not?" Kaila asked nagging and whining.

"It's top secret!" chuckled her mom..

Suddenly there was a squeak… a very faint noise. Looking down at her lap, Breana leaned over and peeked into the basket.

"Oop! Ooops!" Breana mumbled to herself.

"Get out of there, quit peeking!" Sheree harshly warned, catching her in the act as she glimpsed into the rear view mirror out of the corner of her eye.

Kaila now had the basket on her lap and she could feel something wiggling around in the basket as it bounced on her lap. Her brain was racing as fast as her heart was ticking, trying to guess what it could be?

"It surely isn't candy because I think it might be moving and chocolates don't move! Huh, I'm way off base this time."

"What can it be?" Breana contemplated.

"Mom, I think it's moving!" Kaila added.

"It's doing, WHAT? Moving? Kaila, are you sure?" Sheree questioned.

"Uh, huh. Positive! Do you know what it is?" asked Kaila.

"I have an idea," said Sheree.

"I know, it's a rabbit to replace Grapesy who died last year," Breana replied, sounding very positive.

"No, I don't think so-oo! Grandma would not go out and buy another rabbit. She was too heartbroken over Grapsey... But who knows!" Sheree shrugged her shoulders.

"Humm…Besides, you can't replace an animal with another one. They're all different in personalities and each one unique in itself."

Breana's mind continued to spin like a twirling top…imagining what it could be…

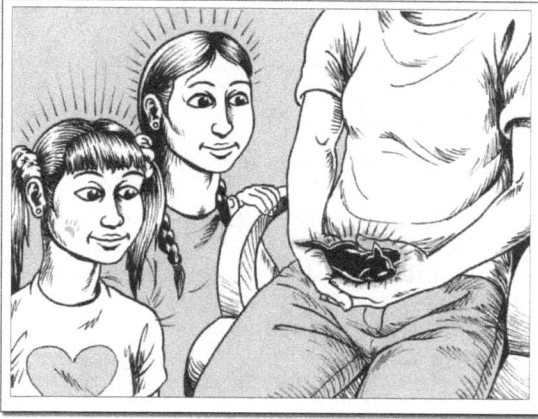

A BIRTHDAY KITTEN
VI

Sheree's driving was always slow and cautious, but today was different. Keen anticipation made her drive erratically. At first, she did not notice the critters that stopped and stared as she drove by. The little tan lizard that was halfway up the front wall of a building stopped dead in his duties and stared intently as the car passed by. Then turning the corner, Sheree saw a big brown dog that took time from his sniffing and scrounging to come out to the end of the alley to have a look. His big sloppy lips wrapped around a piece of hardened pizza. Then a pair of quails flew overhead to land on top of the telephone wires, peering down as she drove toward the park. The cat beneath the park bench rolled over in time to make certain they passed safely. A pair of squirrels paused from chasing each other, sat up, and almost seemed to be saluting. A swarm of vultures circled the area and swooped down toward the car. The little fellow in the basket lay motionless, oblivious to certain phenomena going on in the outside world. Maybe they sensed the kitten's dilemma. The animals were on 'status alert' supporting Sheree's cause on this unusual trip.

The first thought that came to Sheree's mind was that they might have been some of the furry friends Guadalupe had rescued previously. However, she had never rescued vultures or quails. Suddenly, she caught a glimpse of something slithering slowly across the dirt road. She tried to focus more clearly, attempting to identify it. She noticed the wedge-shaped head and the brown body, patterned with diamond shapes that detailed the length of its back.

"Oh, no, it's a rattlesnake!" Sheree yelled as she slammed on the brakes. Scree-ee-ch! Screech!

"Oh, my gosh, I barely missed squashing it."

"What a narrow miss!"

"Wow!" She caught her breath and exhaled a sigh of relief.

"I'm glad I didn't hit it."

She thought of how once upon a time, there was a beautiful desert full of life but the coyotes, javelina, quail and other critters had all been pushed out of their environment to make way for roads, houses and malls. The desert belongs to the wildlife, not us! We are the trespassers.

The rough, bumpy road woke her up from daydreaming, bringing her back to reality.

"Okay, we're at Grandma's!" Sheree said.

Kaila climbed carefully out of the truck making sure she did not bump the basket. She waved good-bye to her Mom and together with Breana, the girls walked quickly to the front of the two-story hacienda. Grandma's own sentinel, the towering Saguaro cactus, stood guard on one side of the front porch. This ancient structure had provided shelter throughout the years for many birds. The giant arm of the cactus currently held a family of rock doves nestled quietly in amongst its thorns. Breana had a perfect eagle-eyed view when she peered through her bedroom window.

The girls went spinning through the front door like two ballerinas, in keen anticipation of the mystery that would soon unfold. Kaila peeked underneath the cloth and without warning, she squealed. She hesitated before saying anything.

"I think it's a hamster!...No, a baby bunny!...Well, no, maybe a guinea pig...Wow! I don't know what it is." She shook her head in frustration.

"Grandma, what is it?" Breana clapped her hands, trying to attract her attention.

"Tell us! Tell us!" shouted the girls, jumping up and down, acting like imps that had stepped on an ant hole.

"Why it's a newborn kitten, you silly goose," said Guadalupe laughing as she revealed the big mystery!

"It's a kitten, a baby, so teeny-tiny," exclaimed Breana.

The girls leaned in close to the basket. 'Too close for the comfort of this baby kitten' thought the kitten with his little pea pod brain spinning...

He let out one squeeky meoww.

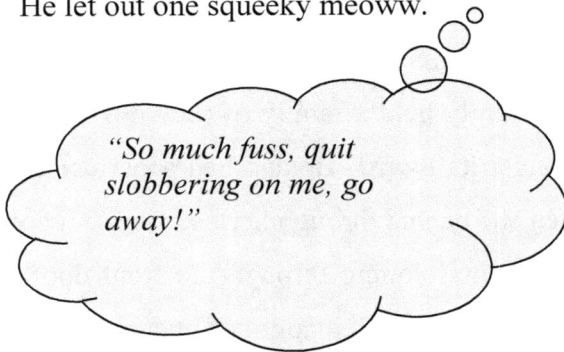

"So much fuss, quit slobbering on me, go away!"

"A kitten? It can't be, I don't believe it," Kaila stammered as she stared at Guadalupe in disbelief.

"Can we hold it, Grandma? Please, Pretty Please," the two of them begged until they heard Guadalupe say,

"Now girls, this little guy is far too young to be handled very much. In fact, Dr. Ingram said he is only a couple of days old. We must always remember to wash our hands 'super duper' clean before and after touching him to protect the little guy, as well as all of us from germs."

With a smirk, the kitten thought to himself,

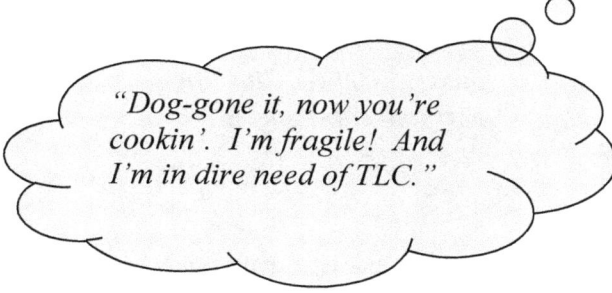

"Dog-gone it, now you're cookin'. I'm fragile! And I'm in dire need of TLC."

"OK! OK!" the girls grumbled, stomping off to the washroom, causing as much noise, if not more, as a stampede of cattle.

Guadalupe took the basket into the living room and set it down gently on the carpet. Peering inside, her heart melted as fast as butter on a hot muffin. The baby tot was squirming around, its nose wiggling, sniffing for its mother.

Guadalupe, overwhelmed with compassion for this tiny creature, squatted down and talked ever so softly, her lips barely moving.

"Don't worry little one, we'll take care of you," she said as she tenderly pet him on the back of the neck, reassuring the kitten. She carefully covered him with a cotton diaper.

The fuzzy little boy kitten seemed to shake his head and say,

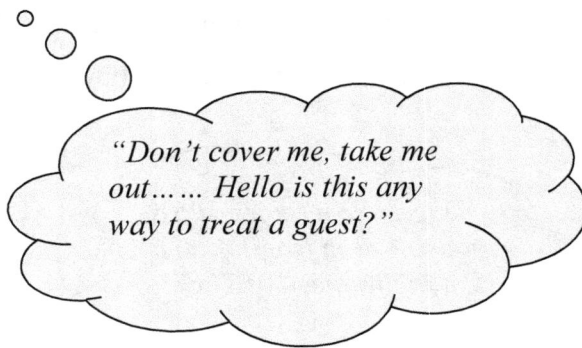

"Don't cover me, take me out...... Hello is this any way to treat a guest?"

No sooner had she stood up when a squeak arose from the basket, which drew Guadalupe's attention. The basket wobbled, swaying far to the left and away from the front door. Guadalupe watched in amazement, as the basket edged away from the door and over to the window. There was no breeze, no marks across the carpet, and no noise.

She smiled and mused to herself. "Yep, there's something going on here." She then felt a cool breeze sweep down past her head. She could almost see the breeze as it distorted the pictures and furniture in front of her as it moved past. Then it was gone and only she and the basket remained.

Guadalupe knew a lot about the history of cats from ancient times and the magical powers they possess. They had the ability to change their environment, maybe even kick up a dust devil when the occasion warranted. Animals were far more perceptive of such things as witnessed by all the critters that watched Sheree's car as she brought the precious basket home. Animals could sense things before humans had the slightest clue—even with all of society's truckloads of technology.

Quick as a wink, the girls bolted back into the room.

"I want to hold the kitten first!" Kaila said eagerly.

"No, I want to! That's not fair!" said Breana.

"You always go first!" said Kaila.

"Do not," exclaimed Breana.

"Do too!" cried Kaila as they argued.

"That's enough! Chill out! You both need to cool your jets. This ruckus will scare the baby kitten. Sit down, relax and we'll talk about it."

"Yes, Grandma," they said sulking, rolling their eyes, as they plunked down beside her.

"Now then," she patted her hands on her lap to gain their undivided attention.

"How are we going to settle this fairly?" asked Guadalupe.

"I know," Kaila spoke up, asserting her typical sensitivity.

"It's Breana's birthday. So she can go first."

Without hesitation, Breana leaped off the couch with excitement.

"Can I, Grandma? Can I really hold him now?" Guadalupe paused for a split second before speaking,

"Well, I don't think it's such a good idea to handle him much, just yet. You can see he is very sick and very weak. We need to take especially good care of him. However, a few soothing strokes on the back of his neck and ears will comfort him.

Breana reached over and petted him tenderly with her fingertip.

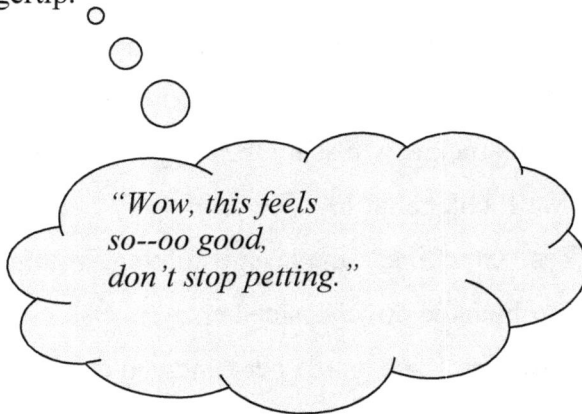

"Wow, this feels so--oo good, don't stop petting."

"Ooooo…He's so fuzzy. What happened to his fur?" Breana asked.

"Baby kittens aren't born with fur, you knucklehead! When the kitten matures its baby fuzz turns into fur," Kaila explained in a superior kind of way.

"Very good, Kaila," Grandma said proudly.

Just then, Sheree came into the house with her husband, Ronald, Guadalupe's son. His bronze colored skin, brown eyes and mahogany brown hair enhanced his subtle good looks. His warm, compassionate manner explained the attraction stray animals had for him.

The trio, Kaila, Breana and Grandma were preoccupied in the living room, jibber-jabbering about Breana's new surprise birthday kitten.

"What's all the commotion?!"

"What's going on? Is everything OK?" Ronald's voice echoed through the hallway.

He walked toward the living room, following the sound of the girls' energetic voices. Kaila greeted her dad with an enthusiastic hug, her hazel eyes glittering like Sheree diamonds. Her half-moon smile punctuated with dimples, lit up her face.

"Daddy! Daddy! Daddy,! She yelled happily, "I want to show you the biggest surprise ever!" She shrieked with sheer delight!

The girls danced and skipped around the room holding hands.

"Look Daddy, look Daddy, isn't our black kitten cute? Her dad glanced down and remarked,

"Dare I ask, what exactly do you have there? Is it a hamster, or a gerbil?"

"No, Daddy, It's a kitten!" Kaila replied sarcastically.

"But it's so tiny and ugly. It looks more like a mouse than a kitten," teased her dad, trying to hold back a laugh.

"Don't you dare say our kitten is ugly? He's only a few days old. I must take extra good care of him! He is very fragile! He has no mommy," Breana rattled on.

The kitten's head sprung up with a meow,

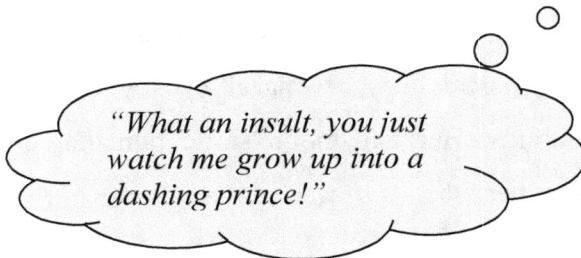

"What an insult, you just watch me grow up into a dashing prince!"

Visions of the past danced in Kaila's mind... 'Simezer, the alley tomcat, didn't have a mother either. He wandered cautiously through the neighborhood searching for food and shelter.'

Sheree peered over Ronald's shoulder, bewildered by this meek, tiny, black kitten curled up in a ball right in the middle of the basket.

"He looks so lifeless and all alone...Poor baby! Poor little boy!" She said sadly.

"Where did you find him?" asked Ronald.

"This kitten, plus one other, was found yesterday abandoned in the cotton bushes near the cosmetic factory in South Phoenix," Guadalupe said, barely able to hide the anger in her voice. Sheree felt crushed upon hearing this!

"Will he survive?" She asked.

"He was separated from his mother far too soon. I am worried about how I'm going to entice him to drink, as his tiny body desperately needs nourishment. He must not dehydrate." Guadalupe sighed heavily...

'Maybe it wasn't a good idea to give this kitten to Breana as a birthday present. What if he doesn't make it and every birthday brings back unhappy memories?' Guadalupe thought about the grim reality that this could

65

have either a happy ending or it could become a dire situation.

"I want our kitten to be happy and live with us forever. What are we going to do?" cried Breana, shuddering and fighting back the tears. She tried to show them all how brave she was, but her lower lip began to quiver. Kaila then burst into tears as she slumped down on the floor.

Ronald felt sad, seeing the sorrow and fear in his little girl's watery eyes but he had every confidence in his mother. He grew up witnessing all the times she had attempted to save animals, and she usually managed one way or another to save them. Ronald knew his mom would teach the girls exactly what to do. He sat down beside his daughter and put his hand on her shoulder reassuring her.

"Don't worry Honey, everything will be okay." Ronald said in a soft voice. "Grandma will save our new family kitten, I just know it!"

Guadalupe knew she had her job cut out for her, but she also knew the risk was worth the valuable lesson that the girls would learn from it. 'Life is worth fighting for… Life is too precious…The power of love will persevere.'

Kaila and Breana feeling a little more optimistic about the kitten, embraced one another as Breana raised her voice. "Let's give our black kitten a name. Let's call him Simba. He is as tough as nails! We'll help him beat all the odds!" With a 'high five' handshake, the girls felt a lot better.

Guadalupe's determination to save Simba grew more intense by the hour and the burning sensation swept through her like wildfire. She knew persistence would eventually prevail, but the fight was just beginning.

What was in store for this baby kitten?

FEEDING WRINKLE

VII

"Kaila! Breana!   Please come here?" cried Guadalupe.

In less than a second, she could hear their feet stomping on the hardwood floor as they quickly approached.

.   "Let's get cracking! I need your help. First, go find me a shoe box and a soft clean cloth," Guadalupe exclaimed.

The girls hurriedly left the room. They scurried through the house swirling like a tornado, destroying everything in its path.

"Ah-ha! Here's a box with my new tennis shoes," declared Breana excitedly!

"But it still has your new shoes in it," Kaila noted.

"So what!" snapped Breana, hurling the shoes up into the air.

"Now it doesn't! Now they're gone!"

"Ouch!!! You hit me in the head with one of your shoes," yelled Kaila as she rubbed the bump on the top of her noggin.

" Oops...sorry," Breana apologized.

"We still need a soft cloth. Hey! I know—I've got it!" said Breana grabbing a tee shirt out of her dresser drawer.

"It's perfect, see? It's new and I've never worn it, making that even better than clean. Feel how soft it is, Simba will love it," continued Breana as she handed it to her Grandma.

"Gracias, mis queridos nietos," said Guadalupe in her Spanish tongue. She reached for the tee shirt, swaddling the kitten in the soft cloth, placing him gently in the shoebox.

"This will keep him warm and cozy. The next best thing to his mother," Guadalupe said, feeling a bit concerned. The girls smiled as they watched Simba's stomach rise and fall in contentment. He seemed to know that things would be okay.

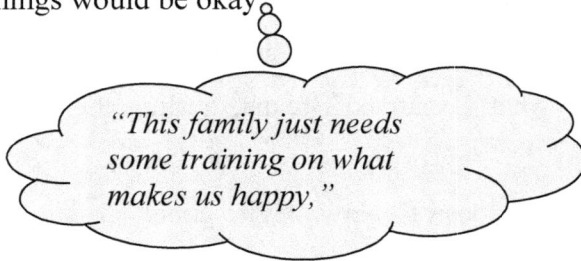

"This family just needs some training on what makes us happy,"

"Now is the time. The time to try and feed him," said Guadalupe.

"How Grandma?" Kaila asked inquisitively as she fidgeted, anxiously waiting for her to begin.

"With an eyedropper," Guadalupe replied, holding up the dropper for them to see.

"Dr. Ingram already tried using a baby bottle, but Baby Simba began to choke," Guadalupe continued.

"He'll choke again," said Breana.

"No, he won't! I have a special way of feeding him," said Guadalupe.

"I'll try mineral water first to hydrate him. If that works, I'll try my luck with the formula that's made especially for kittens," continued Guadalupe.

The awestruck girls nervously watched over her shoulder, as she cautiously picked up Simba and cuddled him in the soft crook of her arm. Ever so gingerly, she placed the tip of the eyedropper carefully into his mouth and squeezed out a few drops of liquid. The girls waited on pins and needles.... could Simba swallow the fluid without choking?

"Oh, no! He's gasping!" Kaila yelled hysterically.

"I know sweetheart." Guadalupe lifted the spurting kitten upright to keep him from choking.

"Why are you holding him like that?" asked Breana.

"I want to prevent the fluid from filling up in his lungs," Guadalupe answered.

"Now, what are we going to do?" Kaila's voice uttered signs of pessimism.

Just then, Ronald strode into the room.

"Kaila, we're going home now. Grandma has her hands full," he said. "Let's give her space and time to think, so she can figure this out. Besides, you have lots of homework that should have been done earlier."

"Dad, I have to stay here with Simba" Kaila pleaded pitifully.

"Please daddy, pretty please, let me stay." She begged.

"I want to help," said Kaila.

Ronald and Sheree looked at each other and shrugged their shoulders.

"If it is okay with Grandma, I guess its fine by us, but you still need to do your homework," harped her father.

"It's okay with me; I'm sure Kaila will be a big help," said Guadalupe.

Guadalupe surprised Kaila with her approval.

"Breana, I'll be back in a second, I am just saying goodbye to mom and dad," Kaila said in an excited voice.

Guadalupe's front entry had a Spanish-style door carved out of pine accented with bold, black hinges as if it were from the 16th century. An intricately designed door handle required the strength of a firm hand to grasp it. The strong, ornate door winced in pain when pushed open. Kaila kissed them good-bye, leaving behind a shadow of her silhouette against the antique door, as she walked towards Breana's bedroom.

She felt a brush of cold air pass against her bare legs as she walked down the hallway. The chill brought goose bumps to her arms, and caused her birthmark to flare up, radiating a neon glow that illuminated the darkened corridor.

"Wow! What was that?" She looked down expecting to see one of the cats, but she did not see a thing. A moment later, another cool breeze swirled around her calves, like a gentle, slithering invisible creature.

Speechless and afraid to look, she finally overcame her fright and peeked down at her legs. Nothing! Then the chilly breeze swooped around her and she could feel it between her ankles again.

"*I think someone is watching me.*" Her body froze and she could not move! An icy chill trickled down her spine as she pivoted around like a ballerina. From the corner of her eye, she caught a glimpse of a faint shadow drifting toward her. Kaila felt hypnotized by this strange phenomenon. Without warning, she felt frosty air blowing on the nape of her neck, causing her to shiver. Her breath became visible as she panted nervously and a silent mist crept in and slowly surrounded her. All she could hear was her heart thump, a resounding pulse that beat all the way up to her ears. Abruptly with no rhyme or reason, the air changed and she felt enveloped with warmth and love. She had visions of Simezer that still lingered in her mind. Simezer, the homeless alley cat wandered the streets, invisible to the world. He searched for friendship, but found only hardship, until the girls befriended him and took him in. Sometimes in her dreams, she would see Simezer floating in a flurry of clouds surrounded by the boundless sky.

"Simezer, wait, don't go, let me pet you," pleaded her shattered voice.

"I need your wisdom. Please Simezer, please stay with me," she implored.

"Our new kitten is dying, what can I do, my spirited friend?"

"I know you're here to help me. Please help me." Kaila asked again, as she stared at a puff of smoke that floated toward the wall.

She felt her heart skip a beat, along with a flutter and she felt nauseated. She stopped dead in her tracks, feeling her legs wobble like wet noodles. She knew it was Simezer. A quick look again.... but she saw nothing. Whatever it was, it had not scared her.

She glanced down at her wet, clammy hands in which there appeared a white fluffy stuffed animal. It was the softest kitten she had ever felt. It was the color of Simezer.

"How did this kitten get in my hands?" Am I going crazy?" Kaila thought to herself.

"It must be Simezer! He's here with me."

The hallway mirror cast an ocean blue reflection upon her. Her birthmark, always pink or reddish in color, had changed to a deep blue, as she looked closely in the mirror. It had become the color of Simezer's eyes. She felt his presence and was reassured that everything was going to be fine. Now she was sure Simezer had paid her a visit.

She heard Breana scampering down the hallway.

"What the heck took you so long, no time for lollygagging," yelled Breana.

"I just saw Simezer," confided Kaila.

Breana wore a strange look on her face and wondered,

"Has my cousin gone off the deep end?"

Kaila's thoughts of Simezer had not faded despite the presence of the new kitten.

"C'mon Breana! We're goin' to go and find Grandma," she shouted "We gotta' stop those old hags from snippin' Simba's string!"

Breana looked puzzled as she tried to understand what her cousin meant. Recognizing the confused look on her face, Kaila added,

"You know what I mean, something like those old witches that are always casting spells!"

"WHAT!!??!!" cried Breana,

"Kaila - you're talking CRAZY TALK, GIRL! Have you gone completely Berzerk-O? The next thing you know you'll start talking with the animals, just like Grandma!"

"YEP, that's right," cried Kaila with a glistening twinkle in her eyes.

"Now hurry up, Breana! Or else the three fates will cut Simba's life-string.

"Follow me!" she ordered. Her cousin scurried right at her heels, but not before Kaila bumped her bare foot against the door, stubbing her little toe. She gave out a "yell," as they burst into Grandma's bedroom.

Guadalupe sat very quietly, rocking the precious babe, softly singing a lullaby. She was ready to reprimand the girls for their unruly entrance when she saw Kaila's flushed face and puffy, glassy eyes with tears trailing down her cheeks. Guadalupe quickly changed her mind. Another repeat stubbing for Kaila's poor abused toe!

"Grandma, I've got it!" Kaila said, reacting quickly as she handed her the stuffed kitten.

"What on earth am I meant to do with this?" Guadalupe questioned.

"Couldn't we use it to comfort Baby Simba by putting it in his shoebox?" Kaila asked.

"Okay, that sounds like a good idea," agreed Guadalupe before adding, "Here's what we need to do next, somehow we've got to trick Simba into thinking we're his real mommy. Maybe, just maybe, if we stick a little pinky finger into the formula and put it to his mouth, he'll start sucking on it."

Breana grabbed the bottle, removed the top and dipped her pinky finger into the milk,

"Here's hoping for a miracle!" she said.

Crossing their fingers for good luck as they leaned down, she put her pinky into Simba's mouth.

This was the moment of truth, will it work? He would not suck on it, but he did open his itsy, bitsy mouth, just enough for Breana to slip in a few drops. The little kitten happily smacked the formula with his tongue and the baby tot squealed a "Meow."

"His tongue feels weird, like rough sandpaper. It tickles," giggled Breana. The girls' eyes sparked with relief and joy!

"Well done, Breana! Good job!" said Guadalupe.

The girls took turns feeding the kitten intermittently, every 15 minutes. In the meantime, Guadalupe was way ahead of the game. She was deliberating as to whether or not this was going to be an effective way to feed him.

"It's working, but it's not nearly enough formula to nourish," she wondered.

"What else can we do? The kitten must learn the 'suckle reflex motion' which comes naturally when they're with their mother." Guadalupe paced around the bedroom with arms folded.

"What should we do next?" she asked herself. She reached over to pet the kitten for inspiration and right there in front of her eyes she noticed a deep wrinkle between her thumb and first finger. Until now, she felt her wrinkles served no purpose, only to diminish her youthful appearance. Now these wrinkles will give life.

"It's going to work! It's going to work now!" She cried in excitement.

She motioned for Kaila and Breana to look at her hand.

"See these wrinkles on my hand, between my thumb and forefinger?" In reaction to her remark, the girls' eyes sprung cross-eyed at each other. The quirky looks on their faces resembled mischievous monkeys in the zoo. Finally, they peered down at her hand, just to be polite.

"This is it! Grandma, you've finally gone off the deep end, absolutely looney tunes," they cried out loudly.

She ignored their comment and put a few drops of formula on her wrinkle as she called out.

"Please bring Simba to me."

"Alright" said Breana.

Obligingly, she picked up the baby kitten from the shoe box, laying the tiny tot on her lap. Guadalupe gently eased the kitten's mouth into the tiny reservoir of formula. His little nose crinkled as he sniffed inquisitively... Then, he began to suck on her wrinkle, lapping up the formula.

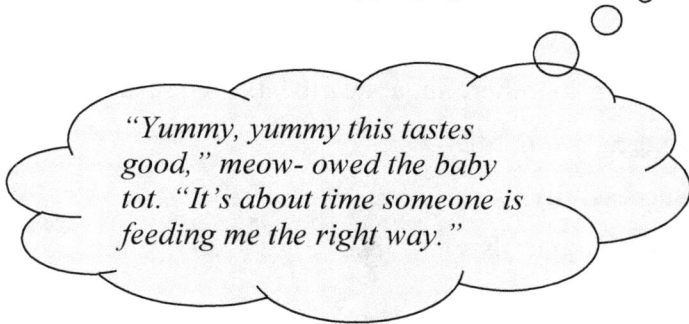

"Yummy, yummy this tastes good," meow- owed the baby tot. "It's about time someone is feeding me the right way."

Without hesitation, Guadalupe placed a few more drops in the wrinkle.

"Grandma, you're a miracle worker," The girls shouted, bursting with joy as their voices bounced off the walls.

As the baby sucked up the milk, they kept adding more, until he had enough and rested his tiny head in the palm of her hand. Finally, her wrinkle served a purpose! Guadalupe thought that old age might be okay after all.

Simba was feeding from a wrinkle.........Wow! Who would have thunk?

Feeling victorious, Guadalupe was relieved the baby kitten fed again during the night.

Guadalupe's face appeared weary and drawn, accentuated with deep gray circles under her eyes that emphasized her laugh lines. She was tired and needed her second wind to kick in.

She remembered the look on the girls' faces the night before, watching their expressions change from despair to relief, in a heartbeat. They had crossed the biggest hurdle successfully. Little could they imagine, this was only the beginning and Simba's young life would be tested for strength  and endurance in the weeks ahead calling on the power of love many times over...

SIMEZER'S MEMOIRS

VIII

Breana was a few paces in front of Kaila and she made a beeline for the living room. The sofa, was just too inviting to pass up. It was their private comfort zone for weary bones. Breana flopped onto the overstuffed cushions and burrowed her way into the pillows, until it felt just right. Raising her arms, she put her hands behind her head and muttered,

"Oh, this is '*so-ooo*' comfy." Her eyelids slowly dropped while her mind drifted back in time to the summer.

"Do you remember last summer?" Breana's sudden question broke the silence.

"Of course I remember last summer. What part of the summer are you talking about?" Kaila asked, as she sprawled out at the other end of the sofa.

"I'm talking about Simezer!" Breana huffed in frustration.

"I can't believe you've already forgotten Simezer."

Kaila, usually a free-spirited person, was always quick to rise and had more energy than she could ever use. Her olive complexion reflected her love for the sun and her hazel eyes sparkled like diamonds. Breana's accusation hurt her feelings causing the paw print on her cheek to gleam a sunset glow.

"I didn't forget!" Kaila defensively snapped back. The two of them had been quietly thinking of Simezer in their own way. Their misty eyes glistened, while their voices stuck in the back of their throats. Memories of Simezer had been etched into their hearts forever. *Cruelty often comes without warning and brings on many questions that have no answers.*

Simezer was a stocky, cream-colored Siamese cat who wandered around the neighborhood at night, sleeping under a mulberry bush directly across the street from

Kaila's house during the day. Scarred and battered from fights with other animals, his abrasions never seemed to heal. His scars showed that his tormentors had no sympathy and he limped around the neighborhood miserable and weary. If anyone came near, he would bow his head down and stagger away, fearful of the human touch. For about a year, Kaila and Breana tried unsuccessfully to coax him to be their friend.

One day, Simezer was across the street when the girls noticed that he held something in his mouth and this sparked their curiosity. They could not make out what he was carrying but Simezer spotted the girls and they exchanged eye contact. He slowly crept across the street heading toward them. They saw him coming closer and closer which shocked them. Breana and Kaila stood still. They tried not to move a muscle as they held their breath. The cat crouched low, his belly almost touching the ground, as he crawled closer to them. Proudly, coming right up to them, he dropped an injured baby sparrow at their bare feet. His luminous sapphire eyes, rich with charisma, enchanted the girls.

They were astonished! Rather than killing this defenseless little bird, his instinct was to protect it. This tough alley cat chose to bring this tiny bird to them. It seemed very strange because no one ever showed any sympathy toward him.

"What motivated him to do this?" The girls wondered....Why? They picked up the baby sparrow and placed it in a rosella bush. The girls sneaked away quietly, hoping its mom would find her little one. This incident with the tomcat inspired the girls to try even harder to befriend him.

With no time to waste, they began making plans to help mend this battered Siamese cat and improve his luck. They felt he deserved a much better life. Most of all, he needed love and loyalty. The two girls being animal lovers through and through, were just the ones to dish it out. They banded together, agreeing he would be their first patient to nurse back to health. They remembered Guadalupe saying that 'experience is the best teacher'.

Kaila sprinted into the house, calling out to her mom. Breana followed close behind.

"Mom, where are you?" She hardly needed to ask as the smell of freshly baked brownies permeated the entire house.

"I'm over here," her mom replied as the two girls started walking down the narrow hallway. They appeared in the kitchen doorway only to see Sheree wearing an apron and oven mitts on each hand, as she took the brownies out of the oven.

"I'm hungry. When will they be ready to eat?" Kaila asked.

"Soon, let them cool off for a bit." Sheree's voice was full of kindness and this encouraged Kaila. Sheepishly, looking at her mom, Kaila pleadingly asked,

"We want to take care of the Tomcat we see wandering the neighborhood. You know the cat we see every day sniffing and rummaging through everyone's garbage."

Kaila, already fearing her mom's answer, thought… "She'll never approve because we have so many animals to feed and care for now." Little did she know…

"It sounds like a great idea!" said Sheree being an enthusiastic animal lover.

She had vivid images of the girls owning their own veterinarian clinic one day. She thought fostering a stray cat would teach them a valuable lesson and strengthen their awareness of the many responsibilities involved in taking care of an abused animal.

That evening, Kaila and Breana put some cat food and water outside on the front porch for the orphan. They decided to call him Simezer, derived from the feline class,

'Siamese,' since he mirrored the reflection of his breed. The girls established a routine, setting a pattern for the tomcat to be fed at the same time every day. Simezer became acclimated to this new schedule quickly. Every night about 7:00 p.m. he cautiously sauntered between the houses, marking a path to his new sanctuary.

Although reluctant at first, he gave up the life of solitude that he had endured for most of his life. The next two weeks whizzed by as the girls focused their efforts on helping Simezer.

Gradually, he became more familiar with the girls by '*hanging loose*' with them. Flirting with them brought him the affection that he longed for and his macho image slowly began to fade away. Weeks went by...when like a bolt from the blue, an amazing twist of fate occurred.

One summer evening after Simezer finished eating he approached Kaila pressing his scruffy body against her bare leg, purring loudly. At first, she was frightened. She froze, resembling a sphinx-like statue. Within seconds, she came to the realization he was looking for affection. The girls were thrilled, and pleased by his gesture.

Eventually, Simezer let other family members approach him, accepting them as members of his 'pack.' He became accustomed to snoozing at Kaila's house in a comfy cat bed, purchased at a garage sale with the girls' allowances. They laid his sleeping pad under their carport to shield him from unruly weather.

Time passed quickly for the girls. Little by little, Simezer's characteristics began to resemble those of a house cat. His scars faded and the abrasions began to disappear. Grooming himself regularly, he had to live up to his new image as 'Casanova!' His fur flourished into a healthy coat, very shiny with a lustrous sheen. He could now strut his stuff with the best of them!

Kaila and Breana were proud! They had rescued an animal all by themselves! Simezer loved being showered with the attention the girls were so eager to give him. His loyalty toward his new family grew more apparent with each passing day. Smothering this once untrusting cat with love and compassion, they had gained a lasting friendship by summer's end. Their triumph was a milestone!

Who could have predicted that a life-changing storm was brewing and this would shatter their faith in human nature, tearing their hearts to shreds?

SHATTERED LIVES
IX

He roamed like an alley cat,

But paced proud, his head high,

Ravaging for scraps of food.

But always enough to give others.

Tomcat being scarred and battered,

But managed to groom daily,

Limped, weary and miserable,

But displayed an aura of dignity.

He had no mother to love him.

But took the place of a mother for other critters.

Life became grim with every passing day,
He always dreamed for a different life.

Little did he know, with each passing day,
The sunrays were becoming brighter.
Suddenly one day, without warning,
His guardian angel appeared brightly.

I have brought forth,
Two loving girls that care,
They will provide shelter,
A comfy bed to sleep.

Your food will be abundant, enough to share,
There will be love and loyalty.
Many sunsets and sunrises,
To greet you in a special way.

His guardian angel asked,
Will you accept my offer.
Telling him, these days will not last,
Simeezer answered with a loud meooww!

Early fall showed signs of cooling weather, as moist dew curled around Kaila's window, beckoning the changing of the seasons.

The uneasy darkness of the night was interrupted with a whip-like wind that shook the old weathered screen window causing it to scrape and rattle. The glow of the crescent moon's face peeking through the stained glass window like a silent warning, glared at her, waking the child. A quiet cry from a vivid dream shook Kaila's sleepy body; her sheets were damp from perspiration. For a moment, she didn't flinch a muscle. Finally, her arm reached out in the darkness feeling for the nightstand next to the bed. Her fingertips lightly touched the light switch on the desert-sand pottery lamp and the bedroom lit up with an iridescent glow.

She sat up in bed, groggy and confused, eyeing the florescent alarm clock hands that glowed 4 a.m. Kaila squinted from the blinding light as she tried to focus, realizing it was still the middle of the night. Coming to her senses, she remembered the worst, most frightening nightmare she just had about Simezer. Kaila's keen intuition sensed something was wrong. This prompted her to check on the Tomcat.

She scrambled out of bed, stubbing her toe on the bedpost. Bravely ignoring the pain, she ran toward the living room. She swung open the front door glancing out into the darkness. The cold air flushed her senses. The moon glowed, casting an illuminating night light on the street below. Kaila stood on the porch as she felt her way along the stucco wall fumbling for the light switch.

"Aah, at last, I've found it!" She flicked on the light. Her voice trembling, she called out,

"Simezer! Simezer! Simezer!" "WHERE ARE YOU?"

Glancing at his empty bed underneath the carport, she had an uneasy feeling. Frantically she looked around the front yard and in the bushes.

"Simezer, where are you!" She rushed back inside the house and raced towards the kitchen, her bare feet tapping on the tile floor. She grabbed his dish and briskly opened his favorite food, a can of tuna fish.

"C'mon, Boy! Here you go," she called out, rushing through the door. "Here's some nice, yummy tuna. He-eere, kitty, kitty, kitty…" She placed the dish beside his sheepskin bed, desperately waiting for him to come home. The ghastly hour passed with no sign of Simezer. Kaila felt sick to her stomach, heartbroken, as she stared at the

Tomcat's bed. Once again, Kaila cried out a quivery wail... Kitt-ty-y. She was tired, her eyes heavy from crying. Her petite body was weak from twitching and shivering,

Exhausted, she curled herself up in a little ball, using Simezer's bed as a pillow, making herself feel comfy. She closed her eyelids to get relief from the burning sensation in her eyes. Her birthmark radiated a hazy red glow.

"Please come, ple-ee-ease, please come back to me...," She whispered, gasping for a breath before sobbing herself to sleep.

The constant sound of rain drumming on the window woke Ronald, beckoning him to save the newspaper from certain drowning. Half asleep, he shuffled outside to the carport, stumbling over his daughter. Startled and surprised, he reached down touching her shoulder gently, waking her from the middle of an unfinished dream.

"Kaila, what are you doing out here?" He asked while staring at the tear stains on her cheeks that emphasized her puffy, bloodshot eyes.

"What's wrong, honey?" He bent down to pick her up.

"Oh, Daddy, Simezer is missing. I had a nightmare about him. When I went outdoors, he wasn't in his bed. I cried so much that I fell asleep here," whimpered Kaila, trembling with fright.

"In my dreams, Simezer wore wings like a bird while swirling like a balloon in the grayish-blue sky. He was drifting into the snowy white clouds with an angel embracing him in her arms. I know something horrible has happened to Simezer! When I came out to look for him, there wasn't a trace of him.. I yelled and yelled until my throat was hoarse. I couldn't yell anymore," Kaila continued.

"Daddy my throat is so dry, it hurts now," she spoke in a raspy voice.

"I even put his favorite food, tuna fish in his dish for him. He still didn't come."

"Don't worry, honey, he's probably roaming the neighborhood like tomcats do. He'll be back when he gets hungry. You know how cats can be. Simezer knows where his food and bed is," remarked her Dad.

He put his arm around her shoulder.

"Honey, let's go inside and warm up," reassuring her the best he could. Kaila agreed and they both walked into the house.

"All right Daddy," but I must call Breana about Simezer.

The morning slowly dragged on…

Their anxiety grew more intense with each passing hour. The faint sun was casting off a golden shower of late afternoon sunlight, a reflection of the desert warmth. Still there was no sign of the Tomcat. Ronald, feeling disheartened, could not shake the uneasy feeling that was swallowing him up. Contrary to his nature, he was undeniably worried. Very worried! Usually a mirror of calmness, he decided to call for action immediately!

"Call out the National Guard!"

"Sheree, go round up the rest of the family for help. Let's do it!" commanded Ronald.

"Let's go find Simezer!" With a 'high five' handshake, they began their desperate search.

Kaila and her father jumped into his 1970 Chevelle, muscle car, the same vehicle he drove in high school. The twosome combed the neighborhood, yielding no results. Feeling exhausted and defeated, they headed for home. There, Sheree had already organized the family members to fan out into special groups but they had no better luck. There was not a clue and not a trace to be found.

Simezer, now officially missing, had become *'The Most Wanted Cat'* in the universe. With their stomachs all tied up in knots, they felt utterly helpless.

"Why can't we find our friend? Why did he leave us? He had such a loving home," Kaila cried.

"Where are you Simezer?" Breana cried out as tears trickled down her cheeks.

"He wouldn't run away from us, we're part of his pack. I know someone has taken him or he's hurt and can't get home," Kaila whimpered.

"Don't worry, I promise we'll find him. Grandma will help; we will not give up. Don't forget she has mystical powers!" comforted Breana.

Guadalupe stared at her son, gesturing him toward the backyard.

"Perhaps Luke, your hound dog could help," suggested Guadalupe.

Luke the mutt dog laid stretched out taking a lazy siesta. He was lanky and pepper-colored with ears so long and floppy, they folded in half like a taco!

Ronald sprang into action. He ran to the backyard and called out Luke's name. The dog looked at him, gazed into his eyes for a moment and yawned— suddenly he jerked his head back and stood upright. His master whipped the leash off its hook, cracking it high in the air. This dopey doggie expression on his face vanished, replaced by a look of keen instinct. The hound sprang into action, his tail a waggin' and thumping loudly against the wall! Luke was ready for some serious action.

"We're off on a cat hunt." Ronald announced as he hooked the leash to Luke's collar. He opened the back door as the hound followed right behind him, howling through the house. He directed him to Simezer's bed.

"Smell that! Smell that real good!" commanded Ronald. Luke pushed his nose into the cat bed, sniffing and snorting, inhaling deeply, until he picked up the scent of the Tomcat. He stood rigid, his nose perked up high, sniffing, letting out a horrific howl.

"Go find him!" ordered Ronald. Luke with intense curiosity flew across the street, bee-lining straight for a large bougainvillea bush. Throwing his head back, he let out an even louder horrendous howl!

"Stay here girls, let me check it out." urged Ronald as he ran across the street where Luke was laying by a hedge, panting and sniffing away. The dog was slobbering over something that looked like a furry animal.

Ronald approached the untrimmed bush cautiously, very slowly as not to scare any critter that might be hiding.

He saw something hairy underneath the dry leaves, as he ordered the dog to move back. Luke refused to obey and continued to whine and sniff aggressively. Bending down on his knees, peering in closely, Ronald discovered Simezer. The cat huddled up in a ball, seemingly lifeless with traces of blood on his cream-colored fur. Simezer, eyes barely open, stared blankly at him. His pleading meow-ooow painfully echoed, "Help me, take me home!"

Ronald's stomach flipped and churned making him feel queasy. He instinctively thought,

"Be careful, don't get too close. Simezer's injuries aren't known and this could cause unpredictable behavior, provoking an attack."

In a split second, this thought disappeared from his mind and Ronald the 'superhero' took immediate action, ignoring all consequences. The only things missing were his cape and tights!

As the girls ran across the street, Luke met them at the curb.

"Daddy, Daddy, Daddy what's wrong?" Kaila cried out,

"Is that Simezer? Is he alive?"

97

"What happened?" Kaila blurted out so many questions that her dad did not know which one to answer first.

"I don't know! He's alive, but hurt!"

Ronald's face creased a deep frown that signaled a strong call for action... "We need Dr. Ingram to look at him immediately," Ronald rasped, expressing tension in his voice.

"Girls, go round up everyone and tell them to meet us at the animal clinic," he shouted in haste. They hurriedly ran back across the street to carry out their mission.

Ronald crouched down slowly and with one hand pulled off his favorite worn out T-shirt. He wrapped Simezer in the soft cotton material. He gently picked him up as a father would his own child. He carried him to the car, shuffling his feet slowly as not to inflict more pain on the cat. Breana and Kaila were already waiting in the car as Ronald laid the cat on the back seat next to Kaila. Simezer was quiet, too quiet, not even a whimper...or even a meow!

Kaila fumbled for her seatbelt, while she stared out the small rear window daydreaming. This was her way of dismissing the blues and the confusion caused by the uncertainty of Simezer's life.

Guadalupe thought 'Cruelty can come without warning, creating an unpredictable outcome. How one's life could be shattered in the mere wink of an eye.'
Driving up to an all-too-familiar place, they arrived at the veterinarian's office. They were greeted at the door before being ushered into an examining room. Dr. Bob, one of Dr. Ingram's associates, gently and tenderly examined Simezer, clearly exhibiting a knack for sensitivity and compassion for critters. In his softest voice and most comforting manner, the doctor explained,

"His right back thigh is wounded and the bone appears to be broken. An x-ray of the leg and thigh will show me the extent of the injuries."

"Okay, take the x-ray," Ronald responded, as he placed his hand on Dr. Bob's shoulder, urging him to listen,

"This cat is no ordinary animal. Our cat had a terrible life in the past. It took a year but the girls finally befriended him. Simezer has shown us that the power of love is a force that can conquer the impossible. Please help him!"

Simezer's meowow, meowow, meowow could be heard throughout the clinic as Dr. Bob whisked him away to the x-ray laboratory.

Time lingered, second by second…minute by minute….the hands on the clock stood still. Worry crept in deeper, taking hold, making every breath a challenge. Gulping down their anxieties, the family huddled together enveloped in a cocoon waiting for the "moment of truth."

Finally, after what seemed like an eternity, the doctor returned with a verdict. He wore a solemn stone-cold look on his face, etched with more than a hint of anger. His expression had a look that could kill.

"Your cat, Simezer has been shot with a .32 caliber gun, causing the thigh bone to shatter," agitation rang in Dr. Bob's voice.

The stunned silence lasted only a moment, and was suddenly broken as Ronald inhaled deeply before speaking.

"I can't believe it." He stomped his foot on the floor! "This has become by far, the worst nightmare imaginable. I had truly grown to admire that cat." Ronald tilted his head down, and ran his fingers through his hair before slipping both hands over his face.

Kaila and Breana were now crying uncontrollably and droplets of tears flowed down their cheeks.

"Why? Why? He was happy with us. We loved him!" They muttered incoherently to themselves.

Ronald stared at Dr. Bob.

"What can be done for him?"

"First we must draw blood to determine if he's carrying any diseases that might affect his recovery," advised the vet.

"Do it!" the apparent anger in Kaila's voice steamed like dry ice in water. Dr. Bob smiled at Kaila, realizing her tone came from grief and despair, making him think, 'It's probably her first experience with the possibility of losing a cherished pet.' He ignored her comment and hurriedly left with the cat, taking him to the lab room.

Time was of the essence now! Reacting quickly could mean the difference between life and death...He returned shortly, his faced anguished, cracked by a deep wrinkled frown. The apparent expression on Dr. Bob's face told the story. The news was not good!

"Simezer has feline leukemia which is usually fatal to cats. It remains dormant until the cat becomes sick or injured. I'm afraid surgery would be the fatal blow," professed the doctor in a saddened voice.

Everyone concerned expressed disbelief. The silence resounded louder than any noise. Guadalupe's voice was faint as she broke the icy silence. The words she spoke saddened all of the assembled family,

"Our only option is to leave Simezer with our dear friend, Dr. Bob."

Knowing what this meant made the heartache they all shared real, very real. Guadalupe knew setting an example would be her most important contribution and maintaining her composure in front of the girls was crucial. Guadalupe thought she was strong and had a grip on herself, but now it was taking all her willpower to keep from crying.

She disguised her feelings by motioning to them, as she put her arms out for the girls. Grandma Guadalupe hugged their stone-like bodies, holding them close. She could feel the vibrations of their sobbing, while warm tears penetrated through her blouse.

"Why Simezer? How can anyone be so mean, cold-hearted and vicious?" The girls asked repeatedly.

"Our tomcat has been very happy with us," reassured Guadalupe. His memories of the last few months were good ones. That's what counts! You knew he loved affection by the way he purred and he finally found a home and a family that cared! Wow, did he ever!" Guadalupe said as she tried to sound a bit more upbeat.

Breana and Kaila took a few minutes to comprehend what they'd heard…

"Simezer was one of a kind, in a class all his own," Guadalupe continued…

"Yes, we are the lucky ones, experiencing the thrill of a wild feral cat that befriended us in his own special way. Simezer fondly showered us with his affection."

Guadalupe looked at the girls and tried to ignore the red outline on Kaila's cheek. She thought to herself,

"Kaila's birthmark must be stinging from all the salty tears," as she watched her scratch it lightly.

"You tamed this maverick to be part of our family. Remember the good times will always remain in our hearts and in Simezer's spirit. We have enriched his life just as he has enriched ours. Never forget that," reminded Guadalupe.

"Poor Simezer; we can't let him see our tears." Sheree said sadly in a heartbroken voice. She wiped the tears from her swollen, pink eyes, which didn't do any good as they just filled right back up again. Sheree walked over to Simezer, unable to look directly in his eyes. She bowed down and caressed him, gently kissing him on the cuff of his neck. The Tomcat's eyes beamed, he squirmed and lifted his head so he could make eye contact with her.

"Don't worry, it's time for my long journey to meet my guardian angel. Listen to my poem," meowed Simezer.

I would rather be loved,
Than not at all by these girls,
I wanted to bring joy into their lives,
Showing them my feelings of affection,

Give them courage to face life,
To go beyond with their love,
When I have gone to a better place,
Let them share loyalty with animal friends,

Thank you my Guardian Angel,
You have made my dreams come true,
I'm waiting for you to take heed,
Finding me an eternal place of compassion,

Floating in the billowing clouds,
With all my other friends,
Will bring so much joy,
I know the moment has come,
Thank you for making my dream come true,

I've shown the girls the way,
To dream and put forth energy,
Believe in one's self,
And see the dreams become a reality.

"I love you," Sheree whimpered, choking back the tears. She quietly left the room, feeling an intolerable sense of loss. Each of the remaining members of the family followed suit. They comforted their dear friend the best way they could, before leaving Dr. Bob to his merciful task.

The somber drive home was unbearable due to their emotionally drained, spiritless moods. The agony of their pain and sorrow left them numb, feeling nothing. Void and empty, they were isolated in silence.

Guadalupe snapped out of her daze, as she glanced at the girls huddled in the back seat. She wanted to hug them and console them in her own way. Breana and Kaila were still too young to understand mortality.

'It's time for a talk about life and death' she concluded.

This grim and sunless day, coincided with their muted mood. Lingering, gloomy, dark gray clouds wallowed aimlessly and the swirling wind threatened more rain.

When they arrived at Guadalupe's home, she herded the girls onto the back porch. She felt the cool air settling in for the evening, as she sat down on the splintered wooden stairs that were in dire need of attention. She motioned to them and patted the spots on either side of her, carefully avoiding the protruding slivers and splinters. After wiping the debris from the steps with her bare hands, they now felt of grit.

"Come sit with me." Breana and Kaila dutifully obeyed, staring blankly into space, expressing despair. They acted more like zombies than two free-spirited girls.

"Grandma, please. Not another one of your lectures, not now." Kaila begged, her head aching like her stubbed toe, still throbbing from the last tragedy. Her birthmark was an added accessory to her pain. The paw print looked like a deep gray bruise and it was sore to touch.

"I'll make it short and snappy," promised Guadalupe. "I truly feel my poem will help you deal with life's expectations and misfortunes. Please listen to the wisdom that comes with my age, I want you to love life and accept death undaunted."

She forced a smile. A trickling of warm tears
sprinkled down her cheeks…

Experience Life Like A Mountain
Climb, Don't Look Back
Your Limits Are High
Expectations Are Met

Rock Edges Are Sharp
Good Pain Brings Appreciation
Sometimes You Stumble
Stumbling Builds Character

Sometimes You Fall
Falling Builds Strength
Death Is inevitable
Treasure Your Memories

Love Is Bountiful
Appreciate Your Life
Commit To One's Self
Dreams Become Reality.

Their roller coaster ride had come to a screeching halt at the top of the incline, but was soon on track again, as it brought on more adventures for the girls...

HOMEWORK MONSTER

X

The day was passing quickly and it was already mid-afternoon. A slight breeze blew through the cracks in the windowsills, making a slight chill in Guadalupe's kitchen. The fading sun shone through the bay window foretelling the approach of evening.

As she stood at the woodstove stirring a pot of homemade chili, Guadalupe began thinking … "An education is so important for the girls, since they're planning to become veterinarians. Studying will be their utmost priority and they'd better get used to it now."

She walked to the foyer and called out to the girls through Breana's closed bedroom door.

"It's time for homework, it's getting late in the day."

"Okay, I'll do it right now with Breana," Kaila answered as she peeked out through a slit in the door.

They shut off the TV and ran out of the room to hunt for their backpacks.

There is never a dull moment in this house. Quiet? Impossible! Guadalupe could hear rumbling and shuffling in the background for several minutes.

"They're suffering from brain freeze, which has short-circuited their memories… causing brief confusion… that's numbed their senses. Par for the course, the girls cannot remember where they put their backpacks. Their heads are filled with oatmeal instead of brains. Their brainwaves indicate a momentary flatline," Guadalupe shook her head.

The backpack hunt was about to begin! The girls were trying to gather their wits together and figure out where they left them.

First clue, the backpacks had been hidden because Grandma did not like seeing things out of place.

"I think I know where they are!" Kaila volunteered.

110

"Where?" asked Breana.

"Let's check the family room." Kaila said.

"Okay," agreed Breana. Off they went, two peas in a pod, bouncing off the walls.

'The homework monster now at large, was seeking out his next victims. The two girls had not done their homework yet! "Hmmm! Hmmm...My work has just begun!" The frightening enforcer exclaimed.

"I see them! Look! I see them behind the couch." Kaila yelled to Breana solving the mystery. The backpacks were exactly where the girls had left them. With backpacks in hand, they marched to the culinary end of the house, cluttering the kitchen table with books.

"It's the pits having school year-round," Kaila protested miserably.

"Get used to it. If we're going to become veterinarians, there's a mountain of books for us to climb" Breana answered back.

Breana and Kaila grumbled under their breath, as they pulled out chairs from underneath the kitchen table. Settling down to an undesirable task and wasting their time on 'homework overload' was against their better judgment. The girls tried hard to concentrate on their schoolwork, only to find their boggled thoughts were wandering off into orbit, thinking about Baby Simba.

Finally, after a few minutes of unwinding, the girls began their assignments. The homework monster had undoubtedly won his battle with the young-uns.

Kaila's eyes lit up as she solved an algebraic equation. While in deep concentration, shapes, sizes, quadrants, and calculations filled her head. Breana continued to study, but Kaila lost patience and she began to chatter incessantly.

"I can't think, much less finish one assignment, with all this going on."

"How can you study when we have a new baby in the house?" Kaila asked.

"Because we have school tomorrow," Breana explained, without looking up from her books. Finally, she gave in and put her pencil down. She started giggling, her laughter was contagious and Kaila's outburst flooded the next room. Breana stared directly into Kaila's eyes before announcing,

"Okay, now we had our fun, let's get back to our homework!"

Time ticked by slowly…finally, an hour passed. In the background, the girls could be heard closing their books with a bang, and a banging, and another bang, signaling a strong indication that homework had been completed under protest.

"What's next?" asked Breana.

"Let's go roller-blading!" Kaila cheerfully suggested.

"Sounds like a winner!" squealed Breana, clapping her hands, jumping up and down as if she were on a pogo stick.

Unbeknownst to the girls, their overabundance of energy was about to be shattered in an instant by a frightening episode.

Unexpectedly a chilly breeze swept through the kitchen as the girls were putting their books away. The stillness of the room foretold a gray sense of death. The noticeable change in temperature bewildered them. Recognizing a supernatural phenomenon was about to happen, their heartbeats quickened and the silence was eerie!

"Are you cold? Breana asked, feeling a frosty chill...

"I feel goose bumps running up my spine. I feel weird, weightless like I am a feather floating in the air.

Look! Look! The walls are beginning to vibrate! Now they're turning to frost!" Breana screamed.

Breana turned pasty-faced, with rubbery arms dangling at her sides and legs that froze in her own footsteps.

"I can feel it! I can feel a presence, a ghost!" stuttered Kaila, as Sherees on her face turned to slivers of ice melting down her neck. She could scarcely breathe, shivering inside her petite frame. Her vocal cords felt tight, very tight and stretched to breaking point.

"Could it be Simezer, our Spirited Tomcat?"

"Can you be real still, like don't move, just freeze?" whispered Breana.

"Maybe, just maybe we'll find out who these spirits are and what they want from us," mumbled Breana's trembling voice as her teeth chattered. She was scared half out of her wits.

"Ghosts are prowling around us! I can feel it! I know they are here! I've read enough ghost stories describing exactly what we're experiencing now", affirmed Breana.

The girls were beyond the point of being scared. They were terrified!

A cool mist with the aroma of spice lingered in the air.

"Look! Look! Look over there toward the corner," Kaila cautioned as she pointed, shaking her finger in that direction. Her heart skipped a beat, then another beat...

"See that grayish shadow floating by the wall?" Kaila continued.

Breana turned her head quickly, trying to catch a glimpse of it.

"It's gone now! You move too slowly," said Kaila, disappointed that Breana had not seen it.

"These spirits could be people we knew once upon a time. Now for some unknown reason, they've come back to pay us a haunted visit," Breana remarked in a monotone voice. A stale, pungent, musty odor now filled the room overpowering the scent of spice.

Kaila started sniffing and gagging all at the same time. "What's that smell?" she asked, trying to hold her breath for a few seconds.

"Breana, I feel sick to my stomach. That smell reminds me of something,...well, you know, Death!!!"

"What do you think?" asked Kaila.
Breana let out a little snicker, as she tried to speak.

"Do you think ghosts wear perfume and smell like roses? They are dead, you know!" Kaila sarcastically retorted.

"This is pretty freaky! Let's get out of this room of spirits," yelled Kaila while biting her lip.

"We're out of here!" cried Breana, forgetting she was the fearless one.

Before they had a chance to leave, a bright yellow light with a neon glow appeared on the wall. It outlined an apparition that temporarily blinded the girls. Quickly shielding their eyes with their hands, they peeked between their fingers, as they watched this form taking on different shapes.

"Wow! It's beautiful! This is awesome! What is it?" Kaila asked.

Although scared by this bizarre image, they felt strangely comfortable. An image of Simezer popped into Breana's head.

"I think Simezer has come back to find his friends. He misses us, just like we miss him." Breana whispered softly.

"I've read that people or animals that die violently must come to peace with themselves. But how do they do this?" continued Breana.

"I don't like this," whispered Kaila, I am scared!

"The spirit makes an appearance by transforming into a ghost-like figure, outlined in a bright light in order for us to see it." Breana explained in a positive way.

The girls looked up at the shadowed wall in the corner of the chilly room and this brought similar thoughts to each of them.

"We love you dearly Simezer. We'll never forget you!"

"Oh never!"

"We miss you, miss you so very much. Please watch over us."

A quick plume of smoke gradually floated toward the far side of the room. The image disappeared into thin air as quickly as it had first appeared.

A feeling of warmth filled the room. The smell of incense, and the coldness vanished. The birthmark on Kaila's cheek started to glow a radiant pink and this cast a shadow of the paw print onto the wall.

Breana and Kaila both in a trance, their skin tingling at the back of their necks, grabbed their backpacks and bolted outside into the garden.

Once out in the daylight, their bones began to thaw and their bodies defrosted. Now was the chance to relax. They exhaled and plunked down on the grass. Their faces were pale, very pale! Staring at each other with saucer eyes, the cold, frigid silence was finally broken.

"Can you believe what just happened to us?" They simultaneously asked each other.

Breana started chuckling. Kaila looked at her strangely, wondering if she was about to lose her marbles.

"What's so funny?" Kaila asked.

"I was thinking about cats and the mysterious attraction they have toward us," Breana said in a mystical voice.

"What do you mean?" Kaila asked.

Breana raised her hand up, pointing her forefinger, using it to count.

"First, Simba catapulted into our lives."

118

"Secondly, Simezer made a ghostly appearance and third, last but not least, were the tigers at the zoo!"

"Remember when we were by the tiger cage?"

"Yes, I remember," grinned Kaila as she continued.

"Those lazy old tigers were taking a mid-day nap at the back of the jungle enclosure. Grandma started making those unusual clicking sounds with her tongue intriguing both tigers. They had been sluggish and tired, but they managed to get up and saunter over to the front of the cage."

"Yeah, that was so cool," Breana added, "Especially when they rubbed their bodies against the bars as if they wanted us to pet them! Were you startled when they let out that roaring purrrr? I know I was," continued Breana.

"Yes, but don't you think it sounded like they were saying, HELLOooo, in tiger talk? That's just too freaky," asserted Kaila.

"You know strange happenings strike like lightning when we're with Grandma, the 'Animal Magnet'. It is like being on a wild, wacky ride with the Energizer Bunny! We just never know what is around the next corner when we are with her." Breana pointed out to Kaila.

"Look at us! We are her two sidekicks! Grandma never knows quite what's in store for her when we're sleeping at her house," laughed Kaila.

"We can be the 'Mighty Pet Patrol,' and Grandma can be 'The Top Dog' because she has bewitching powers!" Kaila explained.

"Breana, do you suppose we'll grow up to be clones of her?"

Breana shrugged her shoulders.

"I'm not sure, but I do know for a fact, she's our mentor and we do spend an awful lot of time with her. It's bound to be contagious."

"Maybe her super powers will rub off on us. I hope so! It sure wouldn't hurt, especially if we become vets when we grow up," said Kaila yawning and stifling a sigh.

"Me too, I'm pooped, let's go inside and kick back for a while." Breana followed suit with a wide yawn.

"Seeing a ghost can take a lot out of you!" Kaila exclaimed, as she shook her head and followed her cousin toward the hacienda.

RAMBUNCTIOUS COUSINS

XI

"Ooooh." What a weird dream!" Kaila moaned, as she sat up in bed.

"It's probably from me sleeping here at Grandma's sanctuary. I am always hearing ghostly sounds that echo throughout the house. The sounds always seem to start at the stroke of midnight."

She looked across the room where Breana was pretending to be asleep. Kaila knew her cousin was faking because she had the comforter pulled up over her head.

"Breana, you forgot to close the shutters last night," moaned Kaila. She closed her eyes tightly, shielding them from the bright glare of the morning sunlight with its rays shining through the window. She felt the warmth tingling on her skin. She imagined this was how a purring cat must feel while being petted.

Kaila was right in the middle of a humongous 'like-From-Los Angeles-to-New-York' kind of stretch, with an equally impressive 'Wide-Open-Swallow-the-Whole-World' kind of yawn, when it dawned on her.

Suddenly a surge of energy rippled through her as she sang aloud and somersaulted off the bed,

"I'm going around the mulberry bush, the mulberry bush"…

"We have a baby kitten! We have a baby kitten to cuddle and love, to care for and watch over! Sim-ba! Sim-ba!" She sang, as she bounced off the walls. Fresh as the morning sun, chipper as a chipmunk! That's Kaila!'

"Be quiet, Kaila! Do you want to wake Grandma?" scolded Breana.

"Wake Grandma up? You must be joking! Are you kidding? Look what time it is," she said pointing to the clock on the wall!

"She's probably been up since five o'clock! You know what she is like, things to do, places to go, people to see and life to live." Kaila rattled on like a broken record.

"Breana, you know how Grandma feels about sleeping at night! Nights are a wee bit too long and a huge waste of time. Cat naps are all she needs" laughed Kaila.

"Get up you blockhead, race you to Grandma's room," challenged Kaila. She sprinted through the house, yards ahead of her cousin, screeching to an abrupt halt as she reached the tall, heavy and firmly closed pair of bedroom doors.

Taking a deep breath, she surveyed the situation.

"Intimidation factor reads past the meter," she dutifully reported, with a mock salute to her Gee-Whiz-Take-All-The-Time-In-The-World-Why-Don't-Ya   newly arrived Comrade-in-Arms.

"Defenses Up?" Breana asked her trusty-dusty first mate in fun.

"Brass-knobbed barrier system, stained glass stare-down security scanner AND....the toe-stubbing, door-jamming ooo-ouch trap-attack-weapon."

"OH NO!....Not the evil toe-stubbing, door-jamming oooo-ouch trap-attack-weapon!   Anything but that!!!"

"It gets us every time!" Kaila solemnly replied, as she looked down at her poor big toe.   It showed signs of black and blue bruising.

"Maybe we should raise our defense shield?"   Breana asked.

"Not in this lifetime! I HATE wearing shoes." Kaila replied.

"Well then, I guess we'd better proceed with caution," Breana said jokingly.

"Agreed, I'll cover the left and you take the right," instructed Kaila as she grabbed the doorknobs. "On the count of three, one-two---threeee"…The great, unyielding doors gave way with a groaning 'cree-ea-ea-k.' The girls crouched down, sneaking in slowly…Shhhhhhhhh.

Guadalupe slyly snuck up behind them, brushing the back of their necks with a feather, and with a loud piercing voice, she yelled "BOO." They jumped up as though they were on pogo sticks, scared half out of their wits. Stifling a chuckle, she captured their little hands and tiptoed with them over to see Simba.

"When can we play with Simba?" Breana asked in a yearning voice.

"Well, Honey, we mustn't let our guard down, just because Simba's health is improving daily.   Without his mother's 'life support nurturing,' there is still a risk of 'sudden death syndrome' during the first three months," explained Guadalupe. Her thoughts were...

'I shouldn't sugarcoat his condition. I should be up front with them, just in case Simba should take a turn for the worse.'

Both the girls were disappointed, but they only wanted the best for Simba. In addition to loving their Grandma, they respected her special knowledge about animals and they had faith that her magical touch would make everything work out for Simba.

But, will Guadalupe's nourishing love be enough to keep Simba alive?

BABY SIMBA

XII

Several weeks whizzed by. Baby Simba, the once meek, hairless kitten was no more. He had grown into Simba, the wild, fierce, growling cat! Yes a wildcat with sharp claws, razor sharp teeth and a tail that thrashed and whipped anything in its path. The latter would prove fatal to anything he came close to, especially insects. Nurtured by humans from birth, he oddly displayed unusual combative and aggressive behavior and his unruliness befuddled the family.

"Grandma, do you suppose Simba is addlebrained?" Breana inquired, inspecting her newest scratch.

"You Gopher-Butt, Simba is not addlebrained!" Kaila yelled.

"See! Not one single mark on ME!" She sneered while showing off her unscathed limbs.

"Well, you're the only one in this house without battle wounds." Guadalupe replied, as she neatly added another bandage to Breana's vast collection. She wore a woven assortment of bandages in every style, color and size imaginable on her arms and Breana looked like a patched up Raggedy Ann Doll!

"I'm not much better!" exclaimed Guadalupe.

"Kaila, I almost forgot, we have a vet appointment in an hour. Will you go and capture our baby beast while I change into a long sleeve shirt? I surely can't go out in public looking like I've just come out of a lion's den."

Guadalupe emerged from the bedroom ten minutes later suitably dressed whereupon she announced,

"Alright warriors, are you ready to go on a perilous venture? Our mission is to take You-Know-Who to the V-E-T. Are you up to the task? Who is the bravest of you two? Who's rising to the challenge of putting Little Simba in his traveler carrier?"

"Aye-Aye, oh Mighty Brave One," Kaila raised her arm forward, "I'm the fearless soldier." Kaila bravely picked Simba up with gloves, putting him into the cage.

Breana eyed Simba cautiously through the wire bars of his prison. Simba glared right back at her with eyes glowing like fiery opals, while he sang his hissing song. "Meoww-w-o-o-ooo."

"Not a very nice song," said Breana shaking her finger.

"I'm not so sure about this. How are we going to take him out of his carrier without any casualties when we arrive at the vet's office?" Breana, the 'worrywart' asked.

"We'll cross that bridge when we come to it," advised Guadalupe.

Simba's meoww, meoowww, meoww serenade, continued all the way to the vet's office.

"Can this get any worse?" Breana exclaimed in an anxious voice. The girls clasped their hands over their ears, ready to disown their little tyke.

She did not have to wait long for her answer. All pandemonium broke out when they entered the vet's office with their little darling. Simba displayed a wild ferocity that no-one thought possible. He growled and roared and then he hissed even louder! Simba was their 'Live Wire' imitating a boom box, complete with Surround Sound, minus the volume controls! He displayed such a highly charged aggression, the rest of the animals in the waiting room simply quaked in terror! The Rottweiler in the corner slunk down, hiding behind his owner. Normally so proud and tall, he was no longer quite so full of himself as a puddle started to form between his legs and he quivered. The German Shepherd across the waiting room, high-tailed it to the door, desperately scratching and clawing to escape.

"Kaila, make him stop! He sounds like someone trying to play a violin without the lessons!" Breana begged.

"How?" asked Kaila.

"Take him out of the cage," said Guadalupe.

Everyone in the room dropped their jaws, as they gazed at her. Probably thinking she's 'one card short of a full deck.' Breana sat and stared at her cousin with apprehension, as Kaila took Simba out of the cage. Kaila cautiously, very cautiously, reached in and grabbed the blanket beneath him. She lifted the edges up around him and slowly pulled the cover out. Then she picked Simba up off the blanket and put him on her lap. Breana reached over and petted Simba, reassuring him that all was 'hunky-dory.'

Silence filled the air as everyone hoped his tantrum was over. Unfortunately, Simba had his own idea. The unfamiliar territory caused him to react in a hostile manner and he did not like this environment one single bit! No indeed-y not in the slightest.

Suddenly, he erupted into the loudest roarrr! Then after some hissing, spitting and growling, he roared even louder than before! The noise was deafening as it bounced off the walls! Simba was behaving like his ancestors in the jungle! 'True to form, he was just like a midget panther,.'

Dr. Ingram ran into the waiting room when he heard all the commotion. His lab coat tails were flying high behind him from the gust of wind he had stirred up as he rushed in.

"Alright, who brought in the whole jungle? I didn't see this scheduled in my appointment book!

Who's making this racket?" he asked jokingly, scanning the room. To his amazement, sitting on Kaila's lap was this tiny, black, green-eyed kitten.

"YOU? It can't be!" Dr. Ingram exclaimed, pointing toward the kitten. "And what might your name be?" Breana blurted out, "That's Simba, he is as tough as nails!"

"You're no bigger than the size of a beanie baby," the good doctor said as he scratched his chin.

"So, please tell me, where exactly is it that you store all this noise? I can't seem to understand how it can all fit inside you."

Simba spotted the doctor, staring him down.....but Dr. Ingram showed no fear of animals. He went to pet the little, plucky, panther look-alike. Simba stood tall and assuredly growled, batting at the doctor's hand with one of his itsy-bitsy paws.

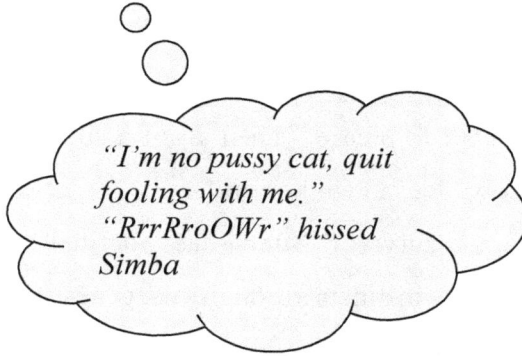

"I'm no pussy cat, quit fooling with me."
"RrrRroOWr" hissed
Simba

"Well Mr. Feisty-face, you are a trouble maker" Dr. Ingram muttered under his breath as he stared down at Simba. Breana nodded her head in agreement.

Dr. Ingram could understand Breana's position by noting the bandages on her arms, and by witnessing the little tot in action.

"Simba definitely has a problem and is in dire need of an attitude adjustment," the doctor expressed his feelings.

131

"Hey Gals, bring me Sweetie-pie."

It was a remarkable sight as they marched in their own little parade and headed towards an examination room. Guadalupe and Breana scurried in front, looking back at Kaila and her cargo, thinking, "How silly we look."

Entering the room, Guadalupe threw her hands up in exasperation, before firing off a number of questions to Dr. Ingram,

"Why, why does my baby act like this? Most of the time, he is a sweet-tempered kitty who loves attention, and he tries so hard to please. Then all of a sudden, his mood swings. Wow, does he go berserk!"

"He's a survivor! Simba has inherited his mother's savage survival instincts through his genes. He has the spirit to live!" The doc candidly replied.

"That's why he survived his ordeal in the desert heat."

"You've all done a great job raising him! It is hard to take a mother's place. However, he has never known another mother, but all of you.

Perhaps Baby Simba visualizes himself as a human and is acting like a spoiled brat," explained Dr. Ingram. "Medically, Simba is fine."

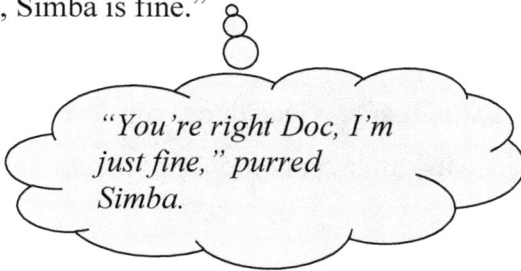

"You're right Doc, I'm just fine," purred Simba.

"Hopefully he'll grow out of this adolescent stage. Be patient!" The doctor spoke with confidence.

"Any questions, call me." He smiled and waved them a good-bye.

Driving home, Guadalupe glanced at her precious baby.

"So, you think you're one of us... Why not?" Stranger things have happened at my house. You'll fit right in," chuckled Guadalupe.

"Young Man, you're definitely a grouch, and a bit rough around the edges," as she shook her pointed forefinger at him, smirking at his innocent expression.

"From now on there won't be any special treatment or privileges, Mister! You will abide by *my* rules. Smarty Pants!" she snarled.

133

"Will you make him take a 'time out' when he's bad?" Breana asked.

"You'd better believe it," said Guadalupe, "Enough is enough."

Nearing home, Guadalupe and the girls tried to gather their wits, after spending a turbulent afternoon with Simba.

It was late afternoon and the weather turned crisp and cool with only a ghost of a breeze.

While Simba catnapped, Breana and Kaila whispered together and coming up with a plan, they crept through the house in a very secretive way. Guadalupe heard some rustling and bustling echoing throughout the casa, originating from the garage. She thought to herself, "What are those mischief's up to now?"

"What is that weird noise I'm hearing?" She wondered.

Whatever it is, I am sure I will find out soon enough. 'Soon enough' came about an hour later.

Suddenly, the door leading from the garage into the house, slammed shut. She could hear the rustling noise of paper in the background, along with unfamiliar loud, scraping noises and then a loud crash and banging against the hallway wall. The girls were hitting furniture and obstacles that crossed their path. A little concerned and somewhat curious, Guadalupe turned and looked in the direction of the noise. A traveling cardboard contraption greeted her.

"Ta-Da!" they popped out from behind the box. Standing very proudly as they unveiled their homemade masterpiece, absolutely beside themselves with delight. They stared and laughed heartily, as Guadalupe inspected the mysterious creation. With a mischievous look, eyes wide open and lips tucked in, the girls announced,

"All of Simba's discipline problems are about to be solved! Now, if he misbehaves, we can send him to his custom-made, time-out box."

"Time Out Box!" yelled the girls simultaneously laughing and giggling helplessly, as they stared at their creation.

Guadalupe and the girls turned their eyes toward the unique cathouse, speechless for a moment and beaming the largest smiles ever.

"Seeing is believing!" Guadalupe said as she admired the patchwork cardboard box. The box was the size of a pet carrier, decorated with various colored stickers that kids collect. It had several holes for windows and packing tape somehow held it all together. What a

remarkable sight, Simba's very own miniature 'Alcatraz!'
Only the best for Baby Simba!

"Do you think he'll like it?" giggled Kaila.

"Let's go find out!" shouted Breana.

"Help me carry the cardboard jail into Grandma's room." The girls hauled it into the master bedroom, placing it down near the door. Simba, being curious, followed them crawling slowly behind the girls. Simba meowed, o

"What 'goo-bots' you are, playing games with me again."

"Guess what we made you, Baby Simba?" Breana playfully teased, as she tapped her fingers on the top of the box, attracting his curiosity. Simba pounced over to the girls' invention, sniffing every inch of it. He was apprehensive at first, which lasted only a few moments. Soon the kitten sauntered inside his box.

"He likes it!" Kaila exclaimed, looking into a peephole in the front of the jailhouse. Bad move! Simba's paw pushed 'thru' the opening, barely missing Kaila's eye. Simba glared out the window at her, as if to say,

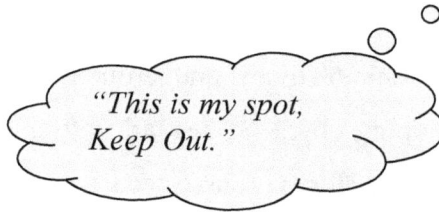

"This is my spot, Keep Out."

"He-ey! If you're going to act like this, you can stay in there!" scolded Kaila.

Ignoring the girls, Simba peacefully coiled himself into a little ball. He flashed a big yawn with a little pout, and faded into a deep sleep.

After an hour catnap, he awoke refreshed, ready for action! He was up to mischief again. Simba jumped out of the 'time out box,' tail swishing back and forth like a windshield wiper. He darted into the living room to hunt down his playmate, Honey, the newest member of the family.

Honey was a rambunctious lab mix. Simba found 'Honey-bunner' (her nickname given by the girls) in the family room, gazing at the deep-green leather couch. This was her very favorite 'chewy' and in no time, the couch had acquired many holes from Honey which were then patched-up with Guadalupe's favorite toy, a hot glue gun. With her tail nervously wagging, Honey started panting in anticipation of trouble from Simba.

Silently, Baby Simba began his game of stalking. He slunk up behind Honey and crouching low, he then pounced, swooping down on her tail with a 'hit and run.' Quick to her feet, Honey 'The Speed Demon' raced after the jungle cat like a lightning bolt. Up and down the hallway, through the kitchen, over couches and into the living room they wrestled and played.

"Honey, you be careful with Simba!" Guadalupe called to her. "You're a giant compared to Baby Simba. Don't you dare hurt him!" Thankfully, Honey had the gentleness of a butterfly.

Reflecting back, Simba had played with Honey since he was three weeks old, very small and weighing less than a pound. Besides, Simba was more than capable of

138

holding his own in any situation that arose with other animals and humans. What a sight to see them play together!

Little did Guadalupe know, there was more to unfold in their lives...

CRITICAL TIME FOR SIMBA

XIII

Weeks went by and all was quiet on the home front. There had been no new additions to the girls' collection of animals. What a relief for Guadalupe. Simba had worn her to a frazzle.

It was late afternoon and the girls were bored with playing the 'Animaloply' game. Kaila looked at her cousin and asked,

"Let's go and find Simba. Do you know where he is?"

"I don't know, let's ask Grandma," said Breana. They skipped into the living room holding hands. There sat

Guadalupe in her rocking chair, reading a book and a mystery novel at that. The shuffling of tiny feet, pitter-pattering into the room interrupted her concentration. She lifted her head and saw Breana and Kaila staring at her.

"What are you girls up to now?" asked Guadalupe as she looked up from her book.

"We're looking for Simba. Have you seen him lately?" Breana quizzed her.

"I thought he was with you," answered Guadalupe, looking a bit puzzled.

"I haven't seen him for hours," said Breana.

"We had better go find him," stammered Guadalupe. The girls ran out of the room.

This is odd, she thought. "Like most children, Simba liked being around people, always seeking attention." Her face crinkled up into zillions of wrinkles showing a deep concern. She placed her book and glasses down.

A few minutes passed when she heard a faint voice calling from the bedroom,

"Grandma, come over here. I found him," Breana called out.

"Did you put him in the 'time out box'?" she asked.

"No," said Guadalupe.

Sure enough, Simba lay in his miniature mansion all curled up, his fur all ruffled and standing on end, looking just like a powder puff. Breana reached down to pet him, talking in a faltering voice,

"He's very warm."

"Let me see," responded Guadalupe reaching down to feel Simba.

It was like touching a warm heating pad. She knew the kitten was sick, very sick. She whipped him up in her arms and wrapped him in a cool wet towel.

"Let's go!" exclaimed Guadalupe. They raced quickly to the car, not looking forward to this trip to the animal hospital.

Greeting them was the familiar sight of the rickety, wood-frame door scarred with many bruises and abrasions. Guadalupe walked through this antique entryway carrying her precious bundle into the office.

"Ladies what's wrong?" Shannon looked up at them.

"Simba is very sick. Can we see a vet right away? It's an emergency!" exclaimed Guadalupe.

"Of course, honey, I'll put you in Cubicle 3" she said leading them down the corridor.

Dr. Murbach was another exceptional veterinarian, who specialized in the care of rabbits and birds, but she also possessed the expertise to help any critter. She recognized Guadalupe's voice, tracking her down in the hallway.

"Uh-oh, not again, let's take a look," said the doctor glancing at baby Simba.

"Follow me." Her tender loving touch and calm personality was capable of putting any ailing animal or distraught pet owner at ease.

Upon entering the room, Breana carefully handed Simba to the doctor.

"Not so bright-eyed and bushy-tailed this morning, are we?" remarked Dr. Murbach as she examined Simba. He let out a pitiful "squeak."

"Simba didn't even come to breakfast this morning. I found him sleeping in his box. His little body was burning up," said Breana. Always on duty, a veterinarian-in-training, Breana listed his symptoms one by one, as the vet listened closely.

"It sounds like he's got a case of 'girardia', (dysentery, like the flu). I will give you antibiotics, but by far the most important thing is keeping him hydrated. We could observe him here if you like, but to be honest with you, he will be better off at home. Besides that, our clinic closes at 6 pm on the weekdays," Dr. Murbach advised.

"Go home. Call me if he doesn't improve in a couple of days."

Guadalupe cradled Simba, petting him behind the ears, reassuring the baby tot that all was well. As fast as they breezed in, they breezed out!

"Grandma, do you believe that cats have nine lives?" Breana asked on the way home.

"Yes, I do! At one time I thought it was a myth, but Simba has given proof that it's true," Guadalupe replied

"Yes, Grandma, I believe it's true! Just look at Simba. I think he just took out another loan from the 'nine lives bank'! Breana started counting on her fingers and then remarked,

"Simba still has several lives on reserve."

Always the optimist, there was no doubt in Breana's heart that a special aura surrounded Simba, guarding and protecting him.

The nights were 'touch and go' and the fears seemed endless. Baby Simba's temperature was far too high and this depleted precious fluids. The ordeal lasted for ten days. The Pet Patrol Trio took turns tending to him, 24 hours a day. Finally, he began to respond and soon he was his old self. He began eating, playing, harassing and displaying his true mischievous tactics. This was a blessing.

But......trouble was only around the corner.

WEEKEND OF FUN

XIV

Time flew by, like a jet's blue smoke streaking across the sky. Labor Day weekend was here!

Kaila and Breana chattered excitedly about the upcoming long holiday weekend. They had their feet propped up on beach towels as they lounged by the kidney-shaped pool, wearing big, dark sunglasses and sipping cherry slushes. Acting like California water babies, they toasted each other,

"It's another holiday! Hall-el-uiah!" Kaila shouted out at the top of her voice.

"And a weekend of fun and living on the edge with, you know who, Grandma" replied Breana.

"I think it is funny seeing her dance around in circles whenever we act like imps," joked Kaila.

"She looks silly when her hair stands on end. Looking frazzled, as though 'Mr. Zap' paid her another visit." Guadalupe's hair served as a stress meter!

"Do you remember playing all those tricks on Grandma last year and seeing who could play the most tricks?" questioned Breana.

"All I know is that I won but you were nipping at my heels the whole way," said Kaila, contorting her face into a goofy expression.

"I know for a fact, yep, it's a proven fact, we can be the most irritating, annoying chimagos (Spanish for children) whenever opportunity knocks at our door," whispered Breana, hoping not to be heard by anyone, especially Guadalupe.

"Boy, we sure kept it up until she was about to flip her lid, didn't we?" Kaila said as she noisily slurped her slushee.

"Kaila, have you ever noticed we can't pull the wool over her eyes for very long? She always seems to be one step ahead of our game," Breana winked, cracking a smile.

"She turns it around and there we are---flat on our faces again. Try as we may, we never seem to get one over on her. I guess we have to admit that she keeps us 'mucho' busy and as she says, this stops us from being troublemakers," chuckled Kaila.

"Aaahh, but look what we get to do," Breana flipped her arms into the air.

Kaila nodded her head in agreement. They were both fantasizing, acting like 'Goobots,' twirling into the pool, splashing water everywhere!

"First we're gonna be Olympic swimmers, and then we'll be soda-slurpin', candy-eatin', popcorn-poppin' girls at the movies. Whoop-ie! Next, we will have sleepovers and play games pretending to be zombies! The next morning we will rise and shine to the aroma of chocolate chip pancakes and bacon, yummy! Yea, that is my favorite breakfast. I could eat them for every meal," Kaila said as she let out a huge sigh, exhaling deeply.

Guadalupe with a slight curve to her lips, smiled as she watched the girls through the bay window while they pretended to be water ballerinas. She leaned out and called to them,

"Hey you mermaids come on inside, it's time to check up on Simba."

"We'll be there in a minute," the girls yelled back.

Some twenty minutes later they nonchalantly trotted in, sopping wet, leaving pools of water behind them.

They found Grandma in the bedroom, preparing for the 5 o'clock feeding.

"Can I feed him, can I please?" begged Kaila.

"He still has a little difficulty eating, maybe next time," answered Guadalupe. Cuddling him into her left arm, she tenderly put the bottle into his mouth. The girls hovered over her, pushing their way for a front row seat.

They watched the kitten eagerly drink from the bottle. Without warning, Simba went limp!

"What's the matter? Something's wrong with him!" screamed the girls.

Still holding him, Guadalupe tried to massage his chest to resuscitate him and said,

"He's not breathing! Call the vet, quickly." In the meantime, she started CPR (Cardio-Pulmonary Resuscitation) while Breana ran to the phone, dialed the number and asked to talk to the doctor.

Breana cried out, "Dr. Ingram said to bring him in immediately."

Guadalupe knew she had to administer CPR continuously but she had no idea how she was going to hold the kitten, breathe into his mouth and push down on his chest intermittently, while driving at the same time. Frantically, she said to herself...

"I have to do this, I must do this to save Simba's life," as she raced to the garage with Baby Simba and the girls fast on her heels. Simultaneously, they all climbed into the car.

"Breana, you will have to hold Simba while I do the driving," said Guadalupe.

"Okay, okay, we'll do whatever you say, please hurry!" replied the girls.

Kaila looked on as Breana was attempting CPR to save the kitten's life. The gravity of the situation frightened them. Their eyes were round and bright, each of them looking like a full moon shining in the black of night. Kaila glanced over at the passengers in the next car and noticed them snickering. It must have looked strange to others, but they did not understand. She rolled down the window and stuck her head out, her hair flapping vigorously in the wind covering her face and making her look like a feather duster.

"Stop it, quit laughing, and quit staring! We're trying to save our baby kitten!" Kaila cried out.

As they screeched into the parking lot, Guadalupe checked Simba and saw that he was gasping for air on his own. They darted into the vet's office as fast as their feet would carry them! It appeared the whole staff, including Dr. Ingram, was waiting to offer assistance. He snatched Simba from Guadalupe's arms and disappeared down the corridor immediately putting the kitten into the oxygen chamber to assist his breathing.

Meanwhile, everyone waited anxiously in the hallway. They eavesdropped, listening for any sound that might come from Simba.

Within minutes, Simba's cries of displeasure rang out loudly, echoing down the passageway. Guadalupe and the girls looked at each other and smiled with relief.

The doctor suddenly reappeared.

"Listen to him, sounds like he's back to his own ornery self. I never thought I'd be so happy to hear that racket again. It's like music to my ears," he chuckled.

"What happened to him?" asked Breana, inquisitively. Dr. Ingram replied with a grin,

"His breathing is back to normal. I suspect he might have swallowed air while sucking on his bottle. Oxygen ceased! Breathing stopped!" The vet explained.

"Simba's 'Special Guardian Angel' sure puts in a lot of overtime!" giggled Kaila.

The Pet Patrol Trio went home with smiley faces, as Simba curled up in a ball on Kaila's lap and fell asleep, snoring very softly. Soon it was nighttime and everyone was in bed except Guadalupe. Her thoughts were floating around in her head as she reflected on Simba's life-threatening episode. It brought back memories of the girl who found and saved the baby kitten from near death.

She thought to herself. "I wonder if she saved any more kittens?"

In the meantime, many miles away...

MIRACLE OF BEES

XV

It was a chilly, blustery day as gray clouds hung low in the sky, brushing the thirsty bare trees with moisture. The bleak day brought forth many sad memories of events that had transpired in Katibelle's past. Yesterday would have been her Mom's birthday. Katibelle slept until late morning, feeling groggy from a restless night of tossing and turning in bed. Her dreams had been full of images of her childhood and she woke up with the sound of her own voice, calling out to her mother.

"Mom I need to hear from you. I have so much to tell you. I miss you. I miss the comfort of being close to you."

As she walked into the kitchen in the late afternoon, the sun broke through the overcast sky for a split second. The brightness of the room created shadows that floated across the paisley tapestry papered wall. Katibelle had an uneasy feeling that someone or something was watching her. Thinking this was silly, she tried to ignore the vibrations that tingled throughout her body. In the far corner of the kitchen, a few feet away, something moved in the gloom, unnoticeable to the naked eye. Moments later, she had that funny feeling again and this made her heart pound rapidly. Her mouth felt dry, just like cotton. Standing at the sink, Katibelle reached to turn on the water, her icy hands looked purple. Looking down at them, she exclaimed,

"What is happening to me, am I going whacko or could it be a real ghost looking for my attention?"

Her senses began to zero in on the sounds in the room, identifying every creak and squeak of her surroundings. Katibelle's intuition finally kicked in as she thought about the white kitten that was hidden in the bush with her brother. The one she had desperately tried to save from death.

Thinking back to that unusual day after work, she remembered finding the two tiny kittens with one being as black as the ace of spades and the other white as snow. The kittens had been huddled in a ball close together as one, so tiny and fragile. She remembered looking down at the two little ones, feeling helpless and thinking,

"How am I going to save these babies?"

"How can one kitten be so jet black and the other one be so snowy white?" she asked herself.

"Surely they hadn't come from the same litter. Why were they together? How did they find each other?"

The sound of the wind soon interrupted her thoughts as the gusty wind swirled around the pillars outside on the back patio. The air was turbulent and chilly. It hissed and moaned through the cracks of the windows and glass arcadia door. Katibelle suspiciously eyed a black, shadowy cloud above the patio. She went to the arcadia door and pressed her nose against the glass when she spied a swarm of bees coming toward her. She thought to herself,

"Why are these bees swarming in this wicked wind during the off season? I remember an old fairy tale that called bees the 'Messengers of Life.' What are they trying to tell me?" She shook her head as she grasped the handle of the glass door and cautiously peeked outside for a better view of the bees. She could hear the throbbing, slow, steady buzzing. Suddenly without rhyme or reason, there was a deafening silence. It was so quiet that you could hear a pin drop. Katibelle had a stark, puzzled impression on her face as she exclaimed,

"Where did they suddenly go to?" There were thousands of them a few moments ago and now I cannot see a single bee. They have just vanished!

"Why? Were they trying to tell me something?" she wondered.

There was a sudden gust of wind that fluttered her hair and she jerked her head back inside.

"Wow" her voice echoed through the kitchen.

Looking out the window she focused on the black oak tree trunk lying on the ground covered with long dry grass. Allowing her imagination to go wild she saw the branches shudder in the wind. The tree reeked of death. Katibelle felt the hair on the back of her neck stand up, causing chills to run up and down her spine. She thought,

"I can feel there's a ghost nearby! Why! Why! Why, am I feeling like this, so strange, so weird? I know I'm a little 'cooky', but I am not insane."

Trying to change her train of thought, she began wondering how the black kitten was adjusting to his new life.

"I hope he's fine in his new home."

156

She thought it was all over. Then a flash of lightning pierced through the kitchen window, lighting up the corner of the room only to reflect eyes that glowed like two coals on the wall. Katibelle looked very carefully at the wall where she had seen the red, beady eyes and she exclaimed in a shivering voice.

"My gosh, what, who are you?"

Her body was limp with fright, as she asked "Mom is that you?"

The silence of the night whispered back. "Purr rr rr." Katibelle let out a sigh of relief.

"Is that you my sweet white tot?" A ghost figure shone on the wall, the image of a baby kitten.

"Is that you, my baby? How are you? Your brother is fine. He lives with a great family that loves cats. He has siblings to play with, but I'm sure he misses you very much," continued Katibelle.

The vision began to fade, but a soft voice meowed,

"I'm fine in this beautiful place, but I do miss my brother. Take care of him, I'll see you all very soon."

Katibelle was happy that the kitten loved her and appreciated that she had done everything possible to save its brief life.

"The bees came to tell me that a friend wanted to relay a message." Imagine that, Katibelle said to herself.

Thinking back in time, Katibelle thought, "I wonder how the little black kitten's luck is holding out?"

She envisioned him as a large, black cat, with tufts on the tips of his ears, his face accentuated with large green eyes.

"I am sure he is probably a beautiful cat now, one of a kind, a survivor." She reflected.

"Hopefully he is he healthy and happy?"

I must find out for sure...

VISIT TO THE VET

XVI

Two months slipped by. Simba was holding his own, coping with the many challenges that threatened his existence.

Simba matured rapidly, his mannerisms increasingly becoming more like a miniature black panther. He was sleek, suave and was just outright gorgeous!

He developed 'tufts', long shreds of hair on the tips of his ears. His lustrous, jet-black, velvet coat enhanced his lean and muscular body. It was just like the story of the frog who magically transformed into a charming prince by the power of love.

It was early morning and Guadalupe sat down to read her mail. She was always busy, an early riser. It was her routine to watch the sunrise launch each new day. Today, being no exception.

She warded off one of Simba's sneak attacks while browsing through her mail at the dining table.

"Hey, Simba, you have mail! Shall I read it for you?" Guadalupe smiled, reaching for her wacky, rainbow-colored glasses. Simba cringed,

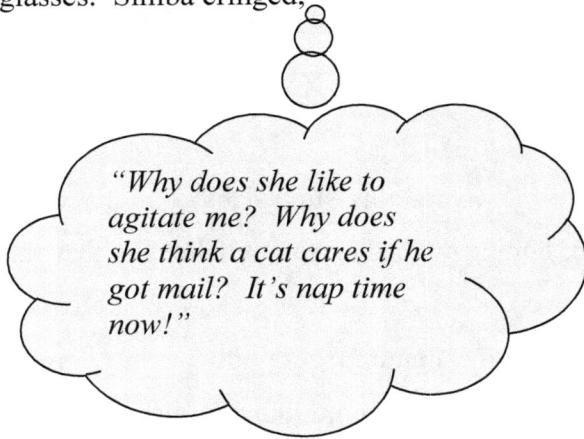

"Why does she like to agitate me? Why does she think a cat cares if he got mail? It's nap time now!"

Simba gave a tiny meow, clawed at the chair, leapt up on the table and grabbed her glasses.

"No damage done little Simba, they're only a buck at the dollar store," laughed Guadalupe.

"Now, where were we? Ah yes, a postcard, an invitation. Oh, it's from your friends at All Creatures Animal Clinic. You are due for your distemper shot. They can't wait to see you again, knowing you can charm them with your lovely voice."

"Well, how about that! Dr. Ingram misses you," smirked Guadalupe. Oh, well..... Hummm.....

"I'd better call and make an appointment for you now, before I forget." Suddenly Simba let out a loud roar.....

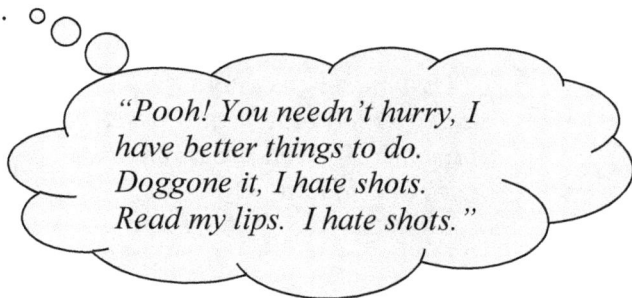

"Pooh! You needn't hurry, I have better things to do. Doggone it, I hate shots. Read my lips. I hate shots."

Later after breakfast, Guadalupe picked up the phone and dialed the number to the vet's office.

"All Creatures Animal Clinic, may I help you?" Shannon cheerfully answered the phone.

"Guess who? It's me." Before Guadalupe could continue, the receptionist replied.

"Hi Guadalupe, what can I do for y'all?"

"It's time to schedule Simba for his distemper shot." Guadalupe said.

161

"You're in luck; my last phone call was a cancellation. Can y'all bring him in this afternoon, the last appointment of the day, 5 p.m.?" Shannon asked.

"Sure thing, I'll be there, thanks," said Guadalupe.

Hanging up the telephone, she turned around eyeing Baby Simba, remarking,

"You're the lucky one. We can see Dr. Ingram late this afternoon. There shouldn't be any animals for you to frighten this time."

"That makes me about as lucky as if a black cat crossed my path," Simba proclaimed with a loud hiss.

With his tail pointed straight up like an arrow, the tip quivered. Simba glared at her with his penetrating, Sheree green eyes before prancing off, acting as if he understood every word she said!

Guadalupe, donned her dark beetle glasses, "Hmmmm....I really should wear glasses that have two arms instead of one. I can't seem to hold onto a pair of normal glasses. Someday I'll splurge and buy a $5.00 pair of glasses, but not today.'

Afternoon soon approached. Guadalupe looked out the bay window in the kitchen and watched the sun peep through under the dark gray clouds that were now over the valley. With the weather looking ominous, she hoped that she would not be caught in a storm when she ventured off to the vet's office.

Guadalupe always wanted to curl up on the couch with a good book to read when a storm approached. And so it was that she picked up a book off the coffee table...

The day seemed to pass by too quickly. Guadalupe put the mystery novel down when she heard the grandfather clock chime four o'clock. It was time to take Simba, the menace, to Dr. Ingram.

"Simba!" she called out firmly. Trotting out of the bedroom, he rubbed up against her.

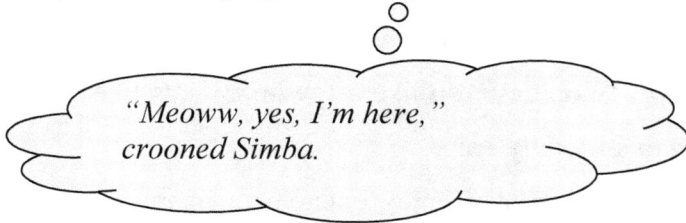

"Meoww, yes, I'm here," crooned Simba.

"It's time to see your friend Dr. Ingram." She picked him up, putting him into his travel carrier quickly, before he had a chance to realize what was happening.

Arriving at the clinic Simba was already on alert, anticipating a sneak attack on all those waiting in the reception area, or so he thought, only to find not a creature was stirring for him to frighten.

Dr. Ingram entered the room. Simba gave the doctor an inscrutable stare, his eyes un-catlike at this moment, were more impressive than ever. If only he could talk like a human. The doctor painstakingly examined Simba despite his attitude. The distemper shot was given hurriedly, while Simba continued his hissing, sassing and biting.

"Simba, you're certainly one of a kind and I'm glad about that! Not even the lion in 'Lion King' could create such a hullabaloo. Your behavioral disposition is in dire need of a fine-tuning," said Dr. Ingram with humor in his voice. He turned his head and smiled at Guadalupe.

"Simba always adds spice to my life. He's made my day." Dr. Ingram placed his arm around her shoulder,

"Wouldn't you like a few more cats like him?" He said in a friendly voice.

"Why not, I enjoy excitement in my life, it keeps me young," Guadalupe gave a chuckle.

"Any concerns?" Dr. Ingram went on to ask.

"Not for now. He's been fine, no problems since his last episode," she said, grinning from ear to ear.

"Good, then I'll see him in a month for his booster shot. Take care." He turned around and vanished from the room.

Guadalupe once again headed toward the door with Simba in tow, thinking, "When will this end?"

"We're on the home stretch, Kid-o." She told him, reaching over patting him fondly behind his ears. He let out a loud meeeeoooow in agreement, 。

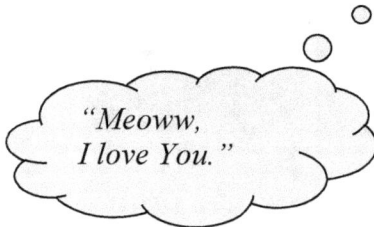

"Meoww,
I love You."

As she drove home she felt somewhat relieved that Simba was finally out of the woods. The raindrops began sprinkling on the windshield, making her think about how life can be as unpredictable as the weather. Little did she know…The unforeseeable was about to show its face…

165

MIRACLES DO HAPPEN

XVII

Not a critter was stirring, not even a mouse! Guadalupe thought this was strange as she called out to Breana.

"You sleepy-head, are you still in bed?"

Breana appeared very tired, looking googly-eyed. Her bewitching hour the night before was the stroke-of-midnight. She rolled over and pulled the blanket up over her head in an attempt to drown out Grandma's voice. Abruptly, Grandma called out again.

"You have an hour to get ready for school!"

"It's not my fault I'm running late," Breana yelled back.

"It's Simba's fault! He didn't wake me up. You know he's my alarm clock."

Breana stretched and yawned.

Guadalupe thought to herself.

"This is very strange" Baby Simba always wakes Breana up in the morning and this is now our regular morning routine...

"Simba, like Guadalupe, was also an early riser. At sunrise, he would begin carousing with the first sign of light beaming in through the slats of the shutters.

One of Simba's favorite past times was bothering Breana early in the morning. Jumping on her bed, he would put his face close to hers, meow-owing' with a rattling purr in her ear, waking her up. If that didn't work, he would pounce, then crawl under the covers, nipping at her toes. Continuing the harassment, Simba would stalk the covers, waiting for that silent movement. Breana would slowly make the covers ripple, provoking an attack.

This would tell Simba that Breana was awake at last. Without any warning, Simba would pounce and this would be the final blow to any thought of going back to sleep! Breana would then peek out from underneath the covers, her eyes half open.

"Simba, thanks a lot for waking me up! It is game time now! Ha, Ha-Ha!" challenged Breana.

As Guadalupe finished replaying the usual morning event in her mind, she could imagine hearing Breana call him softly,

"Baby Simba, come here! I want to annoy you, like you do me." Her icy, stone, voice was enough to send him dashing away, running for refuge to his 'time out' box."

"Where's Simba?" cried Breana, startling Guadalupe.

"I don't know, can you look for him," groaned Guadalupe. Breana soon called back "He's under the bed in the far corner. That is why we could not find him"

Reaching for the little rascal, she pulled him out and immediately sensed something was wrong, very wrong.

"He's sick again," whimpered Breana.

Baby Simba is radiating heat! I think he's almost as hot as a dragon's breath, if that's possible. Oh, Grandma what do we do?"

"Honey, hurry up, get dressed, we must leave quickly," cried Guadalupe as she wrapped the kitten in a cool towel.

They rushed out the door to… guess where?

Running through the doorway of the animal hospital, Guadalupe signed in at the front desk attracting Shannon's attention.

"Oh no, not another emergency?!" exclaimed Shannon.

"Dr. Ingram, get out here quick. It's Simba again!" She called over the intercom.

The amazing Dr. Ingram, quick as a blink, was at her beckoning call. His love for critters was like 'a light from within, that ignited a special glow' when he was around animals.

"Follow me," he said, gesturing them to a room.

Guadalupe put Baby Simba down on the examining table as she tried to comfort him by massaging behind his ears. Dr. Ingram glanced briefly at Guadalupe before diverting his attention toward Simba. He took one look at the kitten and feeling that his stomach was 'hot to the touch' he knew that baby Simba was very sick. He weighed Simba and then took his temperature. The mercury skyrocketed to 104 degrees so fast the doctor thought the thermometer was going to explode!

"Wheww, that's high!" exclaimed the doctor as he turned, arching his eyebrows at Guadalupe.

"We need to give him an injection to lower his fever. By reacting quickly, you probably saved this tiny babe's life. An hour later would have been too late. He's having a reaction to his distemper vaccine which is rare," replied Dr. Ingram.

Shannon, overseeing the situation, came back with a filled syringe. Dr. Ingram administered the fever reduction medication. Fifteen minutes later they all breathed a sigh of relief as Simba's temperature had dropped significantly. Guadalupe's eyes beamed at the doctor for a moment, she asked,

"Can we take him home now?"

"I'm sorry young ladies, he really should stay for the day so I can keep a watchful eye on him. We must monitor his temperature closely. If it elevates again, I'm here to take care of it. Why don't you gals go home and get your beauty rest? When Simba goes home with you, you're going to have to be on your toes, especially at night," warned Dr. Ingram.

They hated leaving Simba there! As they walked out the door, the expressions on their faces, spelled

G - R - I - M.

Breana struggled with the tears that were stinging her eyes and she asked herself,

"Why does everything happen to Simba?"

Guadalupe was upset too, but now was the time to console Breana.

"Dear, we need to be optimistic. He's just too tough! Simba hasn't used up his supply of nine lives yet!" said Guadalupe.

As Breana rubbed the tears from her eyes, a grin slowly crept across her face.

"That's right Grandma, Simba will be just fine."

Breana headed towards the car parked close to the clinic. She looked down as she shuffled her white sneakers on the concrete pavement, causing an irritating, scraping sound. It sent chills down Guadalupe's spine. Under the circumstances, she ignored the noise. This was Breana's way of releasing frustration. Opening the door, she slumped into the car behaving more like a robot than a young lady. Off they went....with somber looks on their faces.

Guadalupe drove home slowly which was not her regular pace, while her mind wandered into another dimension. *'Miracles Do Happen!'*

Suddenly Breana called out,

"What time is it?"

"Half past eight," answered Guadalupe.

"Can you take me to school? I have an exam starting in fifteen minutes."

"Alright, Honey, let's go home and pick up your backpack first" suggested Guadalupe.

"Going to school was a good idea," thought Guadalupe. Occupying Breana's mind would keep her from worrying about Simba."

Arriving back home in less than ten minutes, she pulled over to the curb in front of her hacienda.

"We're home. I'll wait here with the motor running," Guadalupe said to Breana in the backseat. Breana unhooked her seatbelt, climbed out of the car and dashed into the house. She walked out with her backpack, jumped into the car and off to school they went.

"Bye, Grandma. See you this afternoon," said Breana in a quivering voice as they arrived at school. Her eyes showed signs of crying. They were puffy with reddish pink rims.

"He'll be just fine. We'll be picking him up later this afternoon." Guadalupe spoke reassuringly. Breana glanced at her with a hollow expression as she climbed out of the car. Flipping around briskly, she walked toward the school, disappearing in a flash behind closed doors.

Time came to a screeching halt for Guadalupe. Toiling around the house, pacing and feeling emptiness, she could not concentrate. The morning passed at an agonizingly slow pace. She was beside herself, not knowing how her beloved Simba was reacting to the treatment at the medical office. Being dangerously close to having an anxiety attack Guadalupe said to no-one in particular,

"Pacing while eating candy bars is not a pacifier."

Not able to wait any longer, she drove over to the animal hospital around noon, to set her mind at rest. Those antsy feet marched her right into the clinic. From out of the corner of her eye, she glanced at Dr. Ingram. Guadalupe called to him in a rather loud voice,

"How is my Simba?"

"Simba is quiet and his temperature remains normal. I feel he is stabilized!" Dr. Ingram said reassuringly as he approached her.

"Great! I just had to know how he was feeling. Thanks for caring," said Guadalupe.

As this was no ordinary day, Guadalupe had driven her classic Buick to the clinic. Her parents drove this car in the 60's and it brought back happy memories that often supported her in times of a crisis. Guadalupe missed her parents tremendously and she would imagine their presence, as if they were sitting in the car with her. The car had a warm feeling that helped her when the going was tough. In her heart, the 'power of love' keeps the spirits alive and she had a special place in her heart for Alfonso Garcia, her Dad. He was a pillar of the community in Downtown Phoenix where he owned the Southwest's largest furniture factory and store. From the age of six, Guadalupe helped her parents in the store and she knew all the staff and regular customers. With these happy memories, Guadalupe smiled as she hopped into the car. She relaxed against the seat, trying to ease the tension from her body. While she drove, her mind drifted back in time to when she was a teenager. Piece by piece the story unfolded... her first time behind the wheel, feeling so cool! What a priceless thrill! With her Mom in the front seat and her Dad in the back, they tried to teach their spirited daughter how to drive.

Guadalupe spent the rest of the day at home working in her backyard. She looked up at the merciless bright sun in the blue sky while planting flowers to ease her mind. Glancing to the west, she noted that it must be mid-afternoon and time to pick up the girls from school.

She quickly freshened up before racing out of the house with her purse tucked under her arm and climbed into the antique car. Guadalupe approached the school and she could see the girls in the distance, waving their arms back and forth, looking like 'norks' (a cross between a nerd and a dork).

There on the curb sat 'Pencil Legs' and 'Midget Girl', nicknames for Breana and Kaila. They were loaded down with books, anxiously waiting for 'Speed Racer,' their Grandma, to pick them up in her sharp 1968 Buick Special. The body of the car was in mint condition, but it suffered from major mechanical malfunctions. Guadalupe knew a lot about life, but this fountain of knowledge did not include automobiles. The Buick had a mind of its own—it ran as fast as it wanted to run, *when* it wanted to run.

It was not difficult to spot the car in the distance, considering the commotion it created as it sputtered down the street. The sound of the backfire, the burping and

175

lurching as it uncontrollably came toward them. What a sight to see. Puffs of gray smoke brought color to the air. Running alongside the car they laughed and yelled at the same time,

"How's Simba?"

"I think he's feeling much better, but we won't know until we pick him up later," explained Guadalupe.

"Grandma always wears a crash helmet when she drives the old Buick," remarked Breana.

"I think it's dumb! It's stupid!" Kaila said in an exasperated voice, staring at her eccentric Grandma.

"We know you're a little off the wall," Breana offered.

"Do you really find it necessary to wear that crash helmet in public?" Kaila chimed in.

"You're lucky we don't embarrass easily!" said the girls. They loved their Grandma no matter how she came packaged.

Guadalupe glanced back, and with her lead foot, revved the motor,

"Hold on! Put your seat belts on, I'm ready to blast off for home."

The girls braced themselves and buckled up in preparation for another totally cool drive.

Ten minutes flat and everyone was safe at home.

"Another awesome ride!" squealed the norks.

The girls vivaciously skipped into the house and headed straight for the refrigerator, to scavenge for something to munch on.

"We're starving, what is there to eat?" Kaila cried out! Her stomach was always growling furiously!

"There's pizza, cantaloupe and a special treat too." Grandma replied in a chirping voice.

"Yes and Yes, What is the treat?" Kaila asked.

"Rice crispy squares, for my two little angels," she answered with a devilish grin! They were in the microwave, out of Honey's reach; the mischievous dog that eats anything and everything that comes within reach of her nose. Last week Honey ate all the brownies left on the kitchen counter. Her muzzle gave her away with the telltale sign of chocolate crumbs, complemented by the guilty look she had on her face.

"Girls please eat quickly. Do your homework, so we can pick Simba up before they close the clinic," asked Guadalupe.

"Okay! Okay!" they replied.

Breana and Kaila were always in competition with each other, but today they both finished eating at the same time. Doing their tasks together, they made sure they were ready to pick up Simba on schedule. Feeling anxious, their goal was to finish their homework quickly. An hour slipped by when the girls called out,

"Grandma, let's go! Let's go now. Our homework is done!" Guadalupe looked at the clock, thinking it was close enough to 5p.m.

"I'm ready, let's go now!

The girls ran to the car as Guadalupe tried to keep pace with them. She finally put herself in high gear, meeting them at the garage! Rush hour traffic was always an ordeal, not to mention a hassle. For whatever reason, today was different and the trip ran smoothly, allowing them to get there in record time.

Breana and Kaila high-tailed it out of the car and raced to the all-too-familiar entrance.

"I won," said Kaila, as she pushed open the door.

At their own pace, they walked quickly to the back of the office, where Simba was in a cage. Looking in each kennel one by one, Breana spotted their friend first.

"He's over here!" she yelled, pointing her finger towards him.

Simba, eyeing them, sat up and began purring, revving his little motor.

"Take me home! I'm out of here!" pleaded the anxious cat with a deep meow.

"He's alright!" Breana and Kaila jumped up and down, clapping their hands, ecstatic with joy!

Meanwhile, Simba pushed his paw through the wire cage, begging for attention from Kaila.

"Simba wants to play. Look what he's doing with his paw."

"Quit fooling around, let me out, now!" mumbled Simba between his whiskers, staring at the 'norky' girls.

They must have read his mind because Breana opened his cage, handing him to Kaila. They walked to the front of the office where Guadalupe was paying the bill. Glancing at them, she smiled when she saw Baby Simba tucked close to Kaila's chest. Gesturing to the girls, she winked and waved her hand towards the door.

"It's time to go home now," Guadalupe said contently.

"I hope Simba remains healthy for a while," added Kaila. Little did they know, Simba would soon be reaching out for yet another spare life from his guardian angel...

KATIBELLE VOLUNTEERS
XVIII

Clouds billowed in the late afternoon, giving temporary relief from the sun's rays and shedding sprinkles of rain, only for the drops to evaporate in the air before they could hit the ground. However, this was not the monsoon season and it was unusual to see whirls of whipped, puffy, marshmallows in the blue sky at this time of the year. The seasons were not following their usual course this particular year.

Katibelle was now a volunteer at the Humane Society, a rescue facility for unwanted animals. She took a special interest in doing this task because she loved critters and she wanted to make amends for the newborn kitten that passed away at her home earlier in the year. It was a Saturday morning when Katibelle had an appointment with Dr. Ingram. Her latest task as a volunteer was to bring a sick kitten to see the vet. The baby cat had been found in a Quick-Mart parking lot.

Katibelle walked into the vet's office feeling sick to her stomach as it reminded her of the time she brought in the surviving black kitten all those months ago. Katibelle held a small furry ball that was about six weeks old in her arms. Shannon, the receptionist, greeted her at the front desk with a smile,

"Hi Katibelle, I see y'all have another kitten with you? It'll be only a few minutes for a room to open up," Ten minutes passed and then she made eye contact with Katibelle beckoning her to follow.

Moments later, Dr. Ingram entered the room saying,

"I see you're still rescuing helpless critters."

"Yes, I'm still taking care of animals and doing what I do best," Katibelle proudly replied.

"I was wondering what happened to the black kitten that I left with you?" She inquired.

"He survived, but he used several of his nine lives before he was out of danger. It was touch and go for a few months, explained Dr. Ingram.

"Does he have a permanent home now?" asked Katibelle.

"Sure does. He lives with the gal who took care of him when he was critical. They bonded with each other and now they are soul mates. She's now his surrogate mother," chuckled Dr. Ingram. As he put his index finger up to his crinkled forehead, he continued,

"Yeah, Baby Simba became a hero in their household. As the story goes he saved Bacon, their other family cat from near death, when the garage door closed behind her. That day the heat soared well above 100 degrees," Dr. Ingram said.

"Simba cried and nudged the granddaughter's leg with his wet nose prompting her to follow him to the garage. She opened the door and there she found Bacon sprawled on the concrete floor, limp and disoriented from the heat. The Granddaughter cooled her off with a damp cloth. Bacon is fine now, thanks to Simba's quick action!"

"I'm glad to hear a story with a happy ending. I wish I could have taken care of him. I can't handle death very well," Katibelle's voice trailed off in sadness. Her thoughts floated into the past. Often, in the late evening, very tired, but not sleepy, she would flip through the family photo album in bed. One particular picture was of her mom sitting on the couch cradling a special child, which was Katibelle. She would fantasize about her mom flying with white lacy wings, coming to rescue her, embracing her tightly as they floated into the pale blue horizon. Tears would blind her eyes as her lids became heavy and she drifted to sleep.

Dr. Ingram examined the kitten Katibelle had handed him.

"He needs a change of antibiotics. This should do the trick. If he doesn't improve in a couple of days, call me," instructed Dr. Ingram.

"Good-bye Dr. Ingram. I hope *not* to see you any time soon. No offense but I hate to see animals sick," commented Katibelle as she waved good-bye.

Katibelle drove slowly thinking about her mom and all the comforts she has missed. Katibelle dreaded going back to her cottage. She was anxious, feeling butterflies flipping in her stomach and it was as though there was a dark cloud threatening to rain down upon her.

Finally at home, she was greeted with many barks and meows as she walked into her bedroom.

184

The late afternoon cast shadows through the window, causing a hypnotizing spell and soon Katibelle fell fast asleep. Sometime later, Katibelle awoke to the sound of weird loud screeching sounds. She had been dreaming about her mother and the baby kitten she had saved. It was a beautiful dream about the three of them, snuggled together. Still half asleep, the alarm went off signaling the start of another day. She reached for her bathrobe as it was a tad bit cool in the bedroom. Now she was wide awake, she zeroed in on the shrieking echoes coming from the backyard. Katibelle held her breath as she listened intently, focusing on the source. Abruptly, she made a wild dash outdoors, driven by her intuition to follow the sounds. Her eyes focused on the highest branch of a Palomino tree in her backyard. Perched on the highest branch there was a lone black raven, brightly embellished with a fire orange beak. Katibelle was wide-eyed looking at this gorgeous flying specimen. Wondering for a moment,

"Could this be a sign of a bad omen? Is Simba okay? Are there any kittens in distress needing my help?"

Katibelle shook her head in dismay at the chance encounter in her backyard thinking to herself,

"I only see one raven! Where are the rest of them? They're normally in pairs or more."

With eyes fixed on the tree, the whispering breeze gently tossed the branches up and down exposing throngs of ravens. During the night, they had secretly settled deep into the foliage and now the wind had stirred them they began to swarm like bees. They swirled wildly around the trees, acting as though they were part of some unknown phenomenon.

She remembered when she was a small child, about four years old. It was a few days after her mother crossed over the rainbow bridge. Katibelle was in her backyard alone in the playhouse, flipping through a photo album that her Mom had left her. The wind began to blow fiercely, interrupting the silence. She was scared as she inquisitively peeked out the door. High in the mulberry tree branches were shadows of black birds swaying in between the leaves. This scared her so much that she shot back into the play area and scooted underneath the chair she had been sitting on. As a young child, she would wake up from nightmares where hundreds of ravens swarmed around her. She would bat at them with her petite hands and then without rhyme or reason, they would disappear in the swirling wind.

"Why is this happening? This only happens in my nightmares. Normally at this time of the year I only see white doves courting each other." To her astonishment, two ravens swooped very low, so low that she felt the air ruffle her hair. Surprisingly she was not scared, just confused.

"What lies ahead in my future?" I guess time will tell…What do you think?...

ALL OUR ANIMALS

XIX

The doorbell rang, its distinctive chimes echoing through the house.

"Who could this be?" Breana wondered. She walked quickly down the hallway remembering that Kaila was coming over to help with animal chores.

Quick as a flash, she excitedly ran to the door thinking to herself "Oh, good, I have someone to play with now."

Breana heard a thud. This was a well-known warning sound before Kaila's impending entrance. Watch Out! Don't stand in front of the door.

Kaila pushed it open with her banged up bare foot. The door flew open with a 'whoosh' and the ten-year-old yelled,

"I'm here!! Hi, Breana! What's Crankin'?" Breana, being more on the serious side of life said

"Not much, let's do our chores fast, so we can play. Let's make up some fun games today,"

"Where's Bacon?" asked Kaila.

She motioned to Kaila to look in the living room where Bacon was lying on the window ledge.

Bacon was another unwanted, sick kitten, rescued from out of the rain. She was a mellow cat who normally slept on Grandpa's tan, leather chair in the computer room. Kaila did not have to ask about Simba, though. When he heard the bell chime, he ran over to the front door to investigate. Feeling a hairball rubbing against her legs, Kaila looked down at Simba while he purred like rumbling thunder.

"You know how rambunctious Simba can be? He takes advantage of Bacon because of her mellow personality," said Breana.

Kaila burst out laughing.

"Why are you being so silly?" asked Breana.

"I'm thinking about how Grandma reacts when she hears Bacon's loud screaming meows coming from another room as this is a sure sign that Simba is harassing her," exclaimed Kaila.

"I know, Grandma's number one rule, fighting is not acceptable behavior by anyone." declared Breana.

"He's a very smart cat and he understands that fighting with Bacon has consequences. I remember last week, he kept on antagonizing Bacon and he would not let up. Finally, Bacon let out such a loud meow, Grandma came flying down the hallway with smoke ringlets jetting out of her ears. In her rush, she even tumbled and tripped over a plant. Simba's ears were slicked back as he turned towards the sound of her footsteps, immediately taking his chompers out of Bacon's fur, and making a beeline to his cardboard jailhouse for 'Time out," recounted Breana.

"Simba now has a daily routine of seeking refuge in his box when he senses Grandma on the war path" blurted Kaila.

"Do you think our animals are 'dysfunctional' or 'outright smart?" Kaila asked.

"They are outright smart," Breana replied with confidence. "I think we are all tuned in to the same frequency and we can communicate with them and understand their ways as they understand us in kind of the same way"

"That makes sense to me," Kaila exclaimed, mulling over what Breana had just said.

"Look at Simba! Whenever he is locked out of the master bedroom, he rams the wooden door with his body as his paw pushes the handle down. You know how Simba detests closed doors."

"He's smart, a true survivor, genes from a tomcat," Breana's voice said, brimming with pride. She was always reminding Kaila,

"We have the smartest kitten in the world."

"I know that he's a little peculiar like 'you-know-who'? (Grandma) Don't you think so, Breana?" Kaila asked.

Breana recalled the unusual traits Baby Simba had shown and said,

"Do you remember how the sound of splashing water would transform Simba into a mermaid? His ears would perk up at the sound of shower water and his eyes would glow as he ran to the shower door."

"Remember when he was a baby kitten he thought his water dish was a swimming pool. His tiny paws would splash water on the walls, drowning the carpet, soaking whatever was in sight. Don't you think that is a bit strange? Most cats don't like water." Kaila remarked.

"His eating habits are even weirder. He laps up fresh orange juice and chomps on cereal for breakfast. He loves ham, salad, vegetables and fruit. Pizza is his favorite. Let's face it, he's one of a kind, devouring all kinds of human foods. Is he weird or what?" Breana added as Kaila fell about laughing.

"OK, what is so funny now? You're too crazy!" shrieked Breana.

"I was thinking about Hooch, Grandma's large, black and white mutt dog. You know Hooch was always the peacemaker and whenever there was a spat between the pets, he was the referee. It was so funny to watch him rush towards the sound of trouble, and push his stocky body between the animals to break up the fight."

"I can still hear Hooch go ballistic when my Dad teased him and tried to coax him out of the house every time he left Grandma's hacienda. Hooch would use the gruffest voice he could muster up and Dad would always reply, "Okay, big boy, maybe next time you'll change your mind,"

"Fat chance of that ever happening soon," thought the Hooch.

Breana stared at Kaila with glassy eyes.

"I sure do miss our friend," as her voice drifted off...

"Can I sleep over tonight, it's the weekend?" Breana asked.

"It sounds like a great idea to me," Kaila answered, reassuringly. Another new adventure was brewing for the girls...

TENT OUTING

XX

It was early evening. The girls were snuggled in bed with their favorite 'blankie', worn to the nub, chattering away. Their chit-chat mimicked a pair of baby chimps planning mischievous antics. Breana's eyes glowed with excitement at the prospect of freedom and adventure and she suddenly yelled out,

"Let's sleep outdoors in your tent! We're fearless warriors!"

"Great idea! Sounds like a winner to me," said Kaila feeling the anticipation of another 'wild and woolly' scheme.

The girls jumped out of bed, somersaulted on the floor and made their way to the closet. Inside the closet, they grabbed their backpacks, sleeping bags and pillows, and tossed them toward the door. Their second pit stop was the kitchen. This true Mexican cantina often smelled of chili and homemade tortillas and other healthy food, but not tonight as the girls filled their packs with chips, candy and all sorts of junk food.

"Yum, yummy" uttered Kaila. "My stomach is growling. I'm hungry."

The glowing moonlight shone through the windowpane demanding attention. Breana gazed out into the sky; the twinkling bright stars were blinking tiny smiles to their mate, the moon.

Suddenly, glowing eyes that looked like brilliant citrine gems were beaming through the arched window, which startled Breana. She backed away abruptly. Kaila saw this from the other side of the kitchen causing her to snicker and laugh at her cousin.

"It's only Azara, the big bad wolf. She always peeks into the window at night when she sees me or smells food. Azara is going to be our bodyguard tonight," Kaila said in a comforting manner.

"That is great, now I won't be so afraid," said Breana.

Azara would soon be two years old. Her genes carried out every trait of a real wolf to the 'T'. She had a thick double coat, she paced nervously, and she possessed glowing, transparent golden eyes. She never barked, but she could certainly howl. She loved sleeping with the girls and watching over them while they slept. Equally, Breana and Kaila being free spirits, enjoyed sleeping outdoors with their soul mate Azara.

Breana's eyes glittered like diamonds as they made their way outside and with excitement she exclaimed,

"I can't wait to hear the coyotes chattering amongst themselves. We can listen to the owls hooting to their mates. If we're very quiet and very still we will probably hear the insects crawling nearby."

Breana looked at Kaila and thought how hard it was for her cousin to be quiet for one moment and how being still was not one of her strongest traits.

"I'm so happy!" exclaimed Kaila as she stretched her arms high in the air, smelling the wood smoke coming from the fireplace in the casa. She visualized the big mountains encircling the desert and thought of how they resembled ghostly prehistoric dinosaurs. The moon's glow silhouetted some of the tall, bulky boulders on the foothills closer to the house. Kaila began to scare herself when she thought about rattlesnakes slithering into their tent and scorpions dancing outside the tent on the cool grass.

"Stop it," she said loudly, talking to herself.

"Let's put the tent up now. We can then listen to the creatures of the night," cried Kaila in a howling, piercing voice. Squinting her eyes, she made a face like a monster, her mouth stretched open by her two forefingers, trying her very best to frighten Breana.

"That's enough, stop kidding around. I'm not going to sleep in the tent with you, if you keep this up," warned Breana.

"I'm just kidding," Kaila said in a remorseful voice.

Breana and Kaila rummaged around looking for the parts they needed for the tent. They assembled the tent slowly but surely, piece by piece. Finally, the last metal pole snapped into place. The girls were ready to weave the wonders of the night into a memory that they would cherish for the rest of their lives.

"Kaila, you go in first, I'll hold the flap open while you crawl in," said Breana. Kaila was hesitant about being the first inside, but quickly changed her mind. She did not want Breana to think she was a wimp. Bending down, crawling on her hands and knees, she yelled to her cousin.

"Scared-y cat, it's okay, no ghosts, no bugs, you can come in now. Hurry Up!"

"Wait! We seem to be missing certain essential things, like F-O-O-D!" Kaila said in a sarcastic voice,

"Hand me everything that's lying outside of the entrance," she continued.

"Okay, Okay, replied Breana, flinging the backpacks and the other necessities they had collected into the tent.

"Breana, are you coming in now?" asked Kaila.

"I'm coming! I'm coming!" Crawling cautiously, her eyes, big as the size of silver dollars, she inched forwards looking for creepy insects. Breana was still a bit fearful when she entered the tent and she yelled for the wolf dog.

"Azara! It's time to sleep **with** us, you're our bodyguard tonight. Did you forget?" blurted out Breana.

Listening to every sound out in the dark wilderness, the girl's ears were like antennas picking up radar.

"Listen, listen, shhh, be quiet, I hear Azara coming. I hear her paws shuffling through the cool thick grass. She's approaching the tent." Kaila whispered.

"Are you sure it's Azara?" Breana whispered.

Kaila bravely flipped open the flap to the tent and without any hesitation she peered into the darkness.

"Yep, it's Azara! It is not a ghost! Come on in," said Kaila in a smirky voice.

"Good Girl, Azara, you're a good girl, lay right next to me," Breana said as she patted the ground next to her and beamed with delight.

Azara flopped down between the two girls and she curled into a ball with her nose meeting her tail. With deep wolf breaths of contentment, it was obvious to all that she was happy to have company that night.

"Safe at last," thought Breana, feeling a bit relieved.

"Are you still afraid of spiders?" Kaila asked Breana as she noticed a shadow silhouetted by the glow from the moon, crawling on the outside of the canvas tent.

"I'm not afraid of those little creatures," she boasted and laughed loudly in Breana's ear.

"Cut it out, before I go deaf." Breana cried out as she gazed straight up at the ceiling motioning to Kaila.

"What's that crawling out there?" She pointed toward the top of the tent?

"I think it's a tarantula. Let's check it out," Kaila said as she reached for her flashlight. She was always looking for a challenge! Her birthmark began to blush, once again.

Breana was reluctant to leave the tent at first, but went along anyway. They both crept slowly, very slowly, out of the tent. Breana grabbed her light on the way out shining it on the ground, fearful of stepping on a critter, especially a scorpion. Kaila beamed her flashlight on the spider.

"Ugly!" Breana said, as she backed away.

"I think it's a wolf spider!" cried Kaila.

"Yep, I think you're right because it's so big and that yucky thing has hairy legs," replied Breana.

"I should loan him my dad's razor!" suggested Kaila.

"You're really funny," quipped Breana in a sarcastic voice.

"Those glowing eyes are the size of marbles," continued Kaila.

"They're like a mirror," agreed the girls as they bent over for a better look, making sure they kept their distance.

"We can almost see our reflection in those eyes." They exclaimed in unison.

"Watch out!" screamed Kaila.

"He sees us! His back is arching up and the hairy legs are twitching! I think he's about to attack us! They bite, but they're not poisonous," informed Kaila.

"What idiots we are," she thought to herself.

"This is creepy, Kaila! Let's go back inside the tent. This scares me. I feel 'yucky' to my stomach," Breana pleaded.

The girls flipped around and crawled back into the tent where they tried to settle down after their dramatic ordeal.

But they were restless with all the excitement and Kaila spoke in a shivering, eerie voice, "Let's tell stories, how about spooky stories?"

"No," said Breana trying to change the subject, "I want to talk about pets, our weird cat."

"You mean Grandma's 'Watch Cat,' the most fearless cat in the whole wide world, and the smartest cat in town" Kaila said laughing. Simba was indeed the guard cat, always on duty, waiting to pursue any villain that came to the door. When you enter his domain, he might sniff you and perhaps give you a rub on the leg as a cordial gesture if you are lucky. Then he will meow, as he turns away and goes about his business. If his nose is high in the air, this is a warning sign. He is on alert! If his back is arched up high, with straight hairs sticking out along his body and his tail is standing at attention you know he is in control. He has no fear and you would be wise to back away.

"Simba sure doesn't like strangers to befriend him and he always likes to initiate the first interaction, that way he remains 'The Coolest Cat,' yeah, like the one on the Cheetoes bag," advised Kaila.

"You know you're in real trouble when his growl is followed by an open mouthed hiss! Walk with caution!... He's on guard!...Your perpetual shadow!" Breana added.

"You have to admit that sometimes Simba deserves a 'time out,' Alcatraz here he comes!"

The girls continued chatting, laughing and giggling about Simba when Breana asked,

"Remember when Simba met Al. B. Core for the first time?"

"Yeah, isn't he the guy who maintains the saltwater fish tank," answered Kaila.

"I can still picture him when he rang the doorbell. Simba paced and ran quickly to the door like a security guard."

"Simba, sensing Al didn't like cats, showed hostility toward him immediately. We learned later, he hated cats," said Kaila.

"I still can't believe what I saw. Simba without even a warning, only a hissing sound, took a flying leap in Al's direction, catching him off guard. He screamed at the top of his lungs, "Grab That Cat," as he quickly ran into the other room. Grandma couldn't catch Simba because he was long gone, chasing Al. B. Core throughout the house, like some wild cat stalking his prey with intent to kill," Breana trumpeted.

From that point on, Simba was kept in isolation whenever Al. B. Core or other strangers came over.

"Simba's manners leave a lot to be desired," remarked Breana.

The girls shook their heads grinning at each other, always amazed by Simba's antics.

"I still love Simba. He's my Prince Charming. Baby Simba may show his wild side at times, but that shows character" added Kaila.

"Me too," said Breana.

"Simba thinks of me as one of his own, always playing and letting me lug him around like a sack of potatoes. I even fling him over my shoulder while I carry him around. How many cats would let you do that?" Kaila was rattling on.

"None! Simba likes your rough touch because he's a tomcat," said Breana.

"What a sight to watch Tomcat and Kaila play! Simba's purring tickles her, as she 'rough-houses' with him; batting paws and hands, both swinging and flying at each other. Kaila laughs and Simba purrs as they pursue goofball status. They're meant for each other," Breana thought.

Finally reaching a point of exhaustion from all the storytelling it was time for a snooze. The girls unzipped their sleeping bags and slipped inside, snuggling in between the heavy cotton quilting. Glimpses of brown and blonde strands of wavy hair were the only signs of the girls. Azara slept between them, radiating extra warmth. All three were silent when suddenly the two warriors bounced up and still wrapped in their sleeping bags they continued to rattle on again. Kaila whispered to Breana,

"I want to tell more stories, spookier stories, like Grandma's 'bedtime stories,"

"Her true-to-life tales are goose-bump scary. Remember the story she told us about the mannequins she kept in the basement to scare off the ghosts?" asked Kaila.

"How can I forget? Ever since I heard that story, I refuse to sleep downstairs in the basement alone," said Breana.

"Neither will I" said Kaila, with a slight shiver in her voice.

"What bothers me is when the dogs stand at the top of the basement stairs looking down, staring and growling furiously at what? At nothing!" quivered Kaila.

"During the night, sometimes I wake up for no apparent reason and my ears are tuned in for any sound at all. I hold my breath for a second or two, so I can listen, real good...Then it happens! I hear those mysterious echoing sounds coming through the air ducts. To me it sounds like whispering voices, but how could that be?" asked Breana.

"We all know there isn't anyone down there. Dad says that houses make noises from time to time, especially at night when it gets cooler," Kaila added.

"You're scaring me," Breana shrieked, putting her hand over Kaila's mouth who continued to mutter in a muffled voice. Forcefully, her cousin pushed her hand away.

"Why do you suppose those mannequins look like they've been partying all night, their hair messed up as though they had been cruising around in a Cadillac with the top down?" Kaila continued to ask questions.

"I don't know and I don't care! Let's not talk about the ghosts downstairs." Breana's voice, a little shaken, sounded a bit fearful.

Kaila dropped the subject. Blocking it out was her way of dealing with strange phenomena.

Thinking of something different to talk about Kaila then began visualizing Simba wearing a 'cat's eye' stone around his neck, soaring in the air, hunting down hair ties and clips and other hair accessories. He grasped them, flinging them onto a heap. Kaila returned from another galaxy when she blurted out to Breana,

"Have you lost any more hair ties from 'bandido' Simba?"

"Yes, all the time," giggled Breana as she remembered the last incident when she caught Simba carrying around a blue hair bow between his teeth, his tail quivering at attention.

"He looked like a thief making off with the goods."

"Last Monday night, I placed my hair tie on the nightstand. It was missing in the morning. Guess who?"

206

"I found it under the bed along with a pencil and eraser that I'd put on top of my backpack," said Breana crossly.

"To top it off, Simba glanced at me with his evil eye when I scolded him. Then he dawdled between my legs, trotting into the bathroom. Looking so innocent, he stared at me as if to say,

"If you'd put your hair accessories away in the proper place, I wouldn't be tempted to snatch them."

"Can you believe that?" exclaimed Breana.

"You know Simba's favorite past time is collecting hair bows, ribbons, shoelaces and whatever else is available to chew on," said Kaila.

"I know that," agreed Breana.

Breana and Kaila's batteries were running low… their pace slowing down…the sandman was sneaking around, sprinkling sand along the edge of their tent, enticing the girls to visit Sleepville..

Breana tried to fight off sleep, she wished she had two toothpicks to hold her heavy eyelids open, but Mr. Sandman was getting the best of her. Her mouth opened, emitting a big wide 'Grand Canyon' yawn. Kaila followed suit, also yawning, fighting back drowsiness. Kaila rubbed her eyes and mumbled to Breana,

"Do you think I'm normal? Will my birthmark ever go away?"

"You're a very special person! An angel has kissed you. I wish an angel would kiss me and leave a birthmark on 'my' cheek that glowed." Breana reached over and ruffled Kaila's hair, reassuring her that all was fine.

"Enough talking and telling stories, it is 2 a.m. Let's get some sleep," whispered Breana.

The night was still and the coyotes' yelping had fallen silent. There was only the sound of the crickets chirping softly and with this soothing sound, the girls drifted off to sleep - a very deep sleep. You could hear Azara snoring, gruffly ZzzzZzzzzzzz along with the girls' contribution. Grandma always called this 'music' and so the two girls and wolf dog came together in perfect harmony like a choir.

KAILA'S AND BREANA'S MEMORIES

XXI

Kaila and Breana dreamt about floating between the clouds, pillow soft clouds to be specific. Reaching out and stretching their hands, they grabbed at images of animals that needed help. These critters were trapped in a funnel of mystical stars and they cried out for help. Each girl held a kaleidoscope to their eye through which they could see spinning visions of the animals they had saved during their short lives.

They saw Simezer, the Tomcat, whose life had so tragically been cut short. Hooch was the big mutt found crippled, crawling, scavenging for food. Then there was Buddi who was rescued before a car hit him and Zeus who was suffering from malnourishment who was found by their Uncle Cale and Demetria. Simba was the youngest of them all. He became a family member after he was found near death and weighing only four ounces. Whew! There were so many critters in such a short time. How many more furry friends would influence their lives? Each and every one of these unique animals ended up being special gifts.

The sky gradually brightened as the pitch-blackness turned to a lilac-purplish color. The girls woke up to the cool thin light of the early morning filtering through the cracks of the tent's canvas flap door. They grumbled under their breath, feeling very tired from a lack of sleep. Azara awoke feeling restless and she squirmed around, stepping on the girls' feet making them aware that it was time to rise and shine.

"Okay, Okay, we're moving, just wait a second. I'll let you out," said Kaila.

Her eyes were still full of sleep and she had only a slit to see through as she fumbled to find the flap. Opening it up, Azara made her departure.

The girls stared blankly at each other, yawned in unison before sliding back into their dreams. ZZZzzz-zz.

SIMBA

What a twinkle tiny black tot
His Hairless Body, quite a sight
Purring means a kind gesture
Hissing brings on sure fright.

Baby Sim Sapphire eyes look back
Making sure it's safe in the night
His lustrous coat is sleek and black
When it becomes wet, it is such a sight

Baby Sim does not befriend strangers
He carefully watches for them in the night
Strangers put cats in danger
He will stalk at night as the moon shines light.

Baby Sim likes to be canny
But he does not fool granny
He is never afraid of dying
Angels will come and he will be flying.

ACKNOWLEDGEMENTS

I thank my devoted friend Eve Zenoui who has helped pull this book together and encouraged me when the writing was getting tough.

I dedicate this book to all my lovely, free spirited grandchildren Kaila Nicole Knopf, Breana Knopf, Joella Knopf, Jordan Knopf and Lizzy Knopf and to my patient and supportive son Keith Knopf and daughter in law, Sheree Knopf.

A special thank you to Simba who was my inspiration to write this book and who showered me with the spirit of life after all the obstacles he endured during his first year of survival.

None of this would have been possible without the help and support of Jenell Walters who has been my close friend and faithful care giver to all my cats and dogs. Sanela Sinanovic deserves a special recognition for her expert knowledge on saving and treating feral cats.

Special thanks to Zarco Guerrero and Quetzal Guerrero for the wonderful illustrations. Also, thanks to Kyle Ciliento for being such a help to me and to Rick Custance for helping to complete this book and fulfil my dreams.

And not forgetting Azara.

ABOUT THE AUTHOR

Sylvia Knopf is a Phoenix Native and the daughter of Alfonso and Lydia Garcia. The Garcia's had lived in Phoenix long before Arizona became the 49th State and when she was growing up Hispanic families were forced to live in segregated areas as recently as the 1950's. Despite this segregation, the Garcia's ran the largest furniture factory and store in the Southwest and they were renowned for their community support and outreach.

Following her parents' example, Sylvia has created scholarships to help underprivileged teens go to college and supported initiatives to keep kids out of gangs in the inner city neighborhoods.

For many years, Sylvia has poured her considerable energy into animal rescue, and no animal in need is too small or too large. She rescues wild birds and rattle snakes and the fantastic felines in this book were her best friends. They have all helped in their own way to pass her love of animals on to her two grandchildren, Breana and Kaila. She hopes their stories will inspire others to see animals, especially cats, as the unique and loving creatures they are.

All proceeds from the sale of this book will go to animal rescue and care.

www.ingramcontent.com/pod-product-compliance
Lightning Source LLC
LaVergne TN
LVHW051627080426
835511LV00016B/2214